THE
AGE OF
EUROPE

REVISED EDITION

Contributing Authors:
Ira Peck, Elise Bauman

Historical Consultant:

Paul Seaver, Ph.D.
Associate Professor of History Stanford University

SCHOLASTIC INC.

D1377732

Other titles in this series:
The Ancient World
Early Civilizations in Asia, Africa and the Americas
The Modern World

Curriculum Consultants:

William Guardia
San Antonio Independent School System
San Antonio, Texas

Edward Praxmarer
Chicago Public School System
Chicago, Illinois

Helen Richardson
Fulton County School System
Atlanta, Georgia

Staff:

Publisher: Eleanor Angeles
Editorial Director: Carolyn Jackson
Managing Editor: Kevin Gillespie
Editors: Penny Parsekian, Bette Birnbaum, Elise Bauman

Art Direction and Design: Irmgard Lochner
Text Illustrator: George Ulrich
Photo Reseacher: Roberta Guerette/Omni-Photo
    Communications, Inc.
Maps: Irmgard Lochner and Wilhelmina Reyinga

ISBN 0-590-26504-0 (hardcover edition)
ISBN 0-590-34737-3 (softcover edition)

CONTENTS

Great nations write their autobiographies in three manuscripts, the book of their deeds, the book of their words, and the book of their art. Not one of these books can be understood unless we read the two others....

— John Ruskin

MIDDLE AGES: Only members of the court (above) have
time for courtship, or wooing. Outside the castle walls,
peasants till the fields and swim in a stream. Medieval
artists painted biblical characters in impressive
surroundings. "The Birth of the Virgin" (top right) occurs
in a palace. Towns, such as this one in northern Europe
(bottom right), began as places to trade.

RENAISSANCE: Botticelli's "Spring" (detail above), shows Venus and the Mother of Flowers. In Michelangelo's painting (upper left), God gives life to an earth-bound Adam, while Eve peers out from under God's arm. One of the powerful families of Renaissance Italy, the Gonzagas (left) has just learned that a son has been made cardinal.

ITALIAN INFLUENCE: Northern European artists, such as the German, Dürer (left), flocked to Italy to study art, bringing their particular talents with them. The Flemish painter, Van Eyck, in his portrait of an Italian couple (right), includes many personal details of his subjects and their lives. Later, Rembrandt (below), went even further in portraying people in a very personal way.

EXPLORING: Bristol, England (right) was one of the booming European ports that served as a gateway to new worlds of the 16th century. The lure of wealth spurred exploration. John Hawkins, admiral and slave trader (left), found fortune in America. The glitter of coins distracts a banker's wife (below right) from reading her Bible. Early maps (below), were beautiful as well as useful.

ENLIGHTENMENT: *In the 18th century, people enjoyed art (lower left) and the music of Mozart (top left). Inspired by words of philosphers like Rousseau (near left) the National Assembly met on the royal tennis court (above) and pledged to revolt against the French government. Revolutionary leader Marat is murdered (below).*

PART

1

THE MEDIEVAL WORLD

The young knight Roland raised his horn and blew into it with all his strength. He hoped it would be loud enough for the emperor to hear across the mountains. Roland and many other French soldiers were battling desperately against the hostile Muslim enemy. When it became obvious that the French soldiers were going to die, Roland called for help.

Roland hoped that the emperor Charlemagne (SHAR-luh-main) would arrive soon. He wanted Charlemagne to give the dead French soldiers a Christian burial. Roland himself was badly wounded. By the time the emperor arrived, he found Roland's body lying across his sword.

This story is based on one of the most famous legends in French history, *The Song of Roland*. It describes events in the ninth century, although it was probably written three centuries later. Not all the details in *The Song of Roland* are facts. However, the story helps us understand the values of Europeans in the Middle Ages.

As a true Christian soldier Roland was perfectly willing to die fighting people of another faith. He was not calling for support in battle. Such an action would have been a disgrace. But he did not hesitate to summon his emperor to give dead Christians a proper burial. Roland's actions showed a strong religious belief that was typical in the Middle Ages. For this reason, the period is sometimes called the Age of Faith.

What is meant by the term *Middle Ages?* Where did it come from? Apparently, it was first used by European historians of the sixteenth century. They gave that name to the period between ancient times and the times in which they lived. Now the term refers to the years 500 A.D. through 1500 A.D. Another word to describe this period is *medieval* (meed-ee-EE-vul), a Latin word meaning "of the Middle Ages."

It would be wrong, however, to think that the Middle Ages suddenly began in 500. Or that they were over in exactly 1500. Periods of history don't begin or end that sharply. Usually, they blend into one another. In this way, many features of the ancient world lingered into the Middle Ages. Some attitudes of the Middle Ages have even come forward into our own times.

Only the Strong Survived. The Roman Empire in the West had come to an end in 476. For about 500 years after that, waves of invaders swept over much of Europe. The ancient Romans had called such invaders *barbarians* (bar-BEAR-ee-uhns). They were mostly Germanic tri-

18

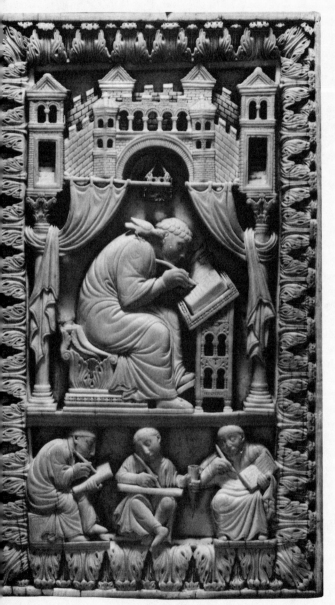

bespeople and had intended to conquer the Roman civilization without destroying it. Yet Roman ideas of law and government were suited to an empire dominated by a city. They could not last in northern or western Europe where there were no cities.

So most of these ideas were soon forgotten. The tribes ruled a Europe broken up into many parts. Each group took its own piece of land. Often, it started fighting its neighbors for their land too. Many features of the Roman Empire—roads, for example —were allowed to crumble away. This early era has been called the *Dark Ages*.

Today historians think that term is not accurate. This is because while the old order was breaking down, a new one was developing. Within the warring kingdoms of Europe, people began to form into groups to accomplish different tasks. The foundations of feudal society were being laid.

The Roman Catholic Church carried over the traditions of Rome into the new age. Its clergy preserved Roman learning and culture. In a time when most people were illiterate, many monks and nuns could read.

Gregory the Great writes his manuscript. Page 16: Ekkehard and Uta, patrons of the Naumburg Cathedral.

19

Most Europeans were converted to Christianity by the ninth century. People came to think of Europe as Christendom (KRISS-en-dum)—the Christian world. Church leaders devoted their whole lives to the Christian faith. Ordinary people also sought to glorify God. Artisans built cathedrals which seemed to reach to the heavens. Others brought scenes from the Bible to life in cathedral windows of stained glass. Some kings even tried to rule according to Christian ideals.

An especially good example was King Louis IX of France. Louis, who lived during the thirteenth century, was a fearless soldier and a just king. But he was also a deeply religious man who followed many of the customs of medieval monks. He wore a haircloth shirt and awoke at midnight to say prayers. He washed the feet of the poor and waited on the sick. Louis was considered such a moral king that he became a saint of the Church.

Throughout the Middle Ages, people went to war over religious beliefs. *The Song of Roland* described such a battle be-tween French Christians and Spanish Muslims.

Muslims believed in the religious teachings of an Arab leader named Mohammed (moe-HAM-ud). Fired by the faith Mohammed gave them, they had spread their ideas to distant lands. By the year 718, Muslims had conquered most of Spain. They even invaded France before being pushed back in 732.

In later years, European Christians fought to regain Palestine from Muslim control. Christians considered the area of Jesus' birth the Holy Land. The wars that resulted were called the Crusades, or Wars for the Cross. They began in 1096 and lasted for two centuries.

The Christians failed, in the end, to rule the Holy Land. But they benefited from their contact with the Muslims of the Middle East. For the first time, large numbers of Europeans traveled in foreign lands. The Muslims taught the crusaders many things. And the Crusades further showed how strongly medieval people were influenced by their faith.

MAP EXERCISE

This map shows some of the more important monasteries, universities, religious centers, and cultural centers in medieval Europe. Use the map to answer the following questions.

1. Name the locations of two universities in medieval England.

2. What is the southernmost center of culture shown on the map? The northernmost?

3. What three universities were located near the Mediterranean Sea?

4. Find the towns of Padua, Albi, and St. Gall. What were these towns famous for?

CULTURAL CENTERS OF MEDIEVAL EUROPE

SCOTLAND

Iona

IRELAND

NORTH SEA

Jarrow

Durham

ATLANTIC OCEAN

Cambridge

Oxford

St. Albans

Salisbury

Canterbury

Cologne

Fulda

Mont St. Michel

Amiens

Aachen

Bec

Laon

Chartres

Paris

Reims

Orleans

Clairvaux

Tours

Citeaux

Cluny

St. Gall

Santiago de Compostela

Albi

Lyons

Bobbio

Padua

CASTILE

Toulouse

Bologna

Montpellier

Florence

Salamanca

Assisi

Toledo

Rome

Monte Cassino

MOSLEM SPAIN

Cordova

Naples

Salerno

MEDITERRANEAN SEA

Palermo

Schools and Universities

Major Religious Centers

Other Centers of Culture

Major Monasteries

Scale of Miles

0   100   200   300   400

21

1
The Merovingian Warlords

It was a time when civilization almost perished in western Europe. The power of government fell into the hands of brutal, plundering warlords. The borders of kingdoms constantly changed with each new battle. Trade ceased, and once-great cities were reduced to towns and villages. Roads crumbled or were swallowed up by forests. Arts and sciences were unknown, except in monasteries. The practice of medicine and just laws ceased. So did public education. Only a few people, mainly monks, nuns, and priests, could read and write. Life was governed by *superstition*. Many events, good and bad, were thought to be caused by ghosts and evil spirits.

Gaul (modern France) was the most civilized region of western Europe after Rome's fall. But under the rule of the Franks, a Germanic tribe, it soon became a savage land. It was divided after 511 into four separate kingdoms. Their rulers were known as the Merovingian (meh-roh-VINGE-ee-un) kings. Although they were closely related, they fought constantly. They murdered, tortured, and plundered to gain their ends.

Much of what we know about sixth-century Gaul comes from the pen of Gregory, bishop of Tours (538-594). His *History of the Franks* gives us a vivid picture of the political and social disorders in Merovingian times. Gregory's education was limited. But he was qualified, by the standards of the time, to write history. As he said, "Woe to our day, since the pursuit of letters has perished from among us."

The following story comes from Gregory's work. It describes a battle between Duke Gundovald and King Gunthram of

A bronze helmet from the sixth century found at a Frankish gravesite

logs tipped with iron] to break down the city walls. But when the soldiers drew near the walls, they were pelted with stones by Gundovald's army. Gundovald's men also threw down pots of burning tar and boiling oil. Many of Gunthram's men died, and his army was forced to retreat.

After another failed attack, Gunthram saw that he could not take the city by force. He sent a secret message to Mummolus, who had once been loyal to him, but now fought for Gundovald. The message said, "What madness possessed you to become a follower of a man like Gundovald? Your wife and your children have been captured, and your sons have already been slain. What do you expect for yourself, except to die?"

Mummolus received the message and replied, "Our power is failing. If you will promise that you will spare my life, I will betray Gundovald and join you again."

Gunthram's messengers returned to Mummolus and said that Gunthram agreed to the bargain. Mummolus then went to Gundovald and said, "You know that I took an oath to be faithful to you. Please take my advice, for I have only your interests in mind. Go outside the city walls and present yourself to Gunthram, who, you say, is your brother. Gunthram's men have told us that the king wants your support, and will not harm you."

Gundovald suspected Mummolus's treachery. He said, "Next to God's help, I placed all my hope in you. And with your help, I always wished to reign as king. If you are lying to me, you will be judged by God."

Mummolus replied, "I am not speaking falsely. Right now, brave men are standing

Burgundy, one of the four Merovingian kingdoms. The duke was trying to seize power from the king by claiming to be his brother. In 585, King Gunthram gained the upper hand in the fighting. His army surrounded Duke Gundovald's men in the walled city of Cominges (ko-MANJ). This is called a *siege*. Gregory wrote:

> The fifteenth day of the siege had come. Gunthram's chiefs began to prepare new weapons to destroy the city. Among them were wagons with battering rams [heavy

outside the gate, waiting to welcome you."

Then they went outside the gate and were received by two of Gunthram's chiefs. Mummolus went back inside the city and barred the gates very securely. When Gundovald realized that he was betrayed, he raised his eyes to heaven and said: "God, from whom all justice comes, I plead my cause. I pray that you punish those who have betrayed an innocent man."

Then he crossed himself and went off with his captors. When they had gone some distance from the gates, one of them pushed him to the ground. The captor shouted, "Here is Gundovald, who says he is the brother of a king." He threw his lance at Gundovald, but it was stopped by Gundovald's armor.

Gundovald rose and tried to flee to a nearby hill. But his other captor threw a stone and struck his head. Gundovald died. His enemies tied his feet with a rope and dragged him through Gunthram's army camp. Then they dragged his body back and left it for the vultures.

Afterward, Gunthram's chiefs plundered the city. Everyone in the city was murdered. Clergymen were killed at the altars of their churches. Then Gunthram's men burned the whole city down.

Meanwhile King Gunthram gave orders that Mummolus be killed. When Mummolus heard of this, he put on his armor and went to see the commander of Gunthram's army. Mummolus protested to him, "I see that you are not going to keep the promise that you made to me." But the commander assured him that he would be allowed to live.

Gold coin showing Frankish king, Theodobert I. He was the grandson of Clovis, the first Christian Frankish king.

Then the commander went out and broke his promise by ordering the house surrounded. Mummolus fought long and hard for his life. Finally he was killed. Then Gunthram's soldiers returned home, plundering and killing along the way.

As we can see, no one in this story could quite trust anyone else. Mummolus promised loyalty to Gunthram, then deserted him for Gundovald. Then he betrayed Gundovald when their army was losing.

Disloyalty Punished. Why was Mummolus killed? He had broken a most important rule: to pledge loyalty to a leader and stay loyal till death. Even though he helped Gunthram take the city, Gunthram killed him because he could not depend on him.

The Merovingian kings were descended from Germanic tribespeople. They were *nomadic*, or wandering people and fought other tribes for property. In a tribe, loyalty to a strong leader was their most important value. Because the world lacked law and order, loyalty was often the only thing that kept people from turning against one another.

With horsemen like this charging Merovingian, the Franks overran the Gauls.

Other Germanic customs still existed in Merovingian times. For example, people accused of a crime underwent *trial by ordeal*. This meant that they would be tested in some way. For example, an accused person might be made to walk on fire. If their wound healed within a certain number of days, they were thought innocent. They might instead be thrown into a lake. If they floated they were considered guilty. If they sank, they were declared innocent. Guilty persons paid a fine or were whipped or mutilated. In some cases they were killed.

Life under the Merovingian kings was far from easy or secure. However, their power could not last much longer. By 800, the Merovingian kings had little real power. Historians now call them the do-nothing kings. Certainly, they did little that would further the cause of peace. The Franks needed a leader to unite them and bring order and justice to the land.

✎ Quick Check

1. *Describe Europe in the sixth century.*

2. *Which part of Europe was considered the most civilized? Who ruled this area? What kind of leadership did they provide? When did their power decline?*

3. *What historian wrote about these times? Who were Gunthram and Gundovald, and why did they fight? Who was Mummolus, and why was he killed?*

4. *The rulers of this period were descended from what people? By what process did they determine innocence or guilt?*

2
To Serve the Soul

How was civilization able to survive the disorders and terror of the early Middle Ages? It happened in a way that no one could have predicted. Small groups of men, dedicating themselves to God, gathered together in religious communities. Set apart from the semi-barbaric world, they became centers of light. Within their walls, they preserved and protected both classical culture and Christian teachings.

These men became known as *monks*, and their communities as *monasteries*. The word *monk* comes from the Greek *monos*, which means alone or solitary.

The first monks were hermits who went to live in the deserts of Egypt and Syria around the late third century A.D. These men wanted to get away from the city and town life, which they considered corrupt. They devoted themselves solely to prayer and repentance for sin. They punished themselves in ways that were often extreme. They ate very little, spent years in silence, refused to bathe or wear comfortable clothes, and sat for days in the heat of the desert sun. One desert hermit, Simeon Stylites, lived atop a pillar for more than 30 years without ever descending.

Gradually monks also began to gather in organized communities where they lived under a common *rule*, or discipline. So, from living alone, monasticism came to mean just the opposite. Monks lived together, but still apart from society.

Monastic life spread rapidly over the Roman Empire during the last century of its existence. But there was very little unity. There were almost as many rules as there were individual monasteries.

Then the greatest of all monastic law-

In the war-torn Middle Ages, monestaries like this one, helped keep education in Europe alive.

givers appeared on the scene. A Roman, he gave to the monastic world the same gift of organization that the ancient Romans gave to the political world. He created a structure that was not only able to survive the disorders of the times. It was eventually able to restore a world that was in physical and social ruin. This Roman was St. Benedict of Nursia. To many people, he is considered the father of western European civilization.

Oddly, very little is known about the life of St. Benedict. His fame rests almost entirely upon his rule. A biography of him written by a pope, Gregory the Great (about 540-604), praises him but contains few facts. It is possible, however, to reconstruct at least the bare bones of St. Benedict's life.

Benedict was born to a prosperous country family in the province of Nursia sometime around 480. This was soon after the last Roman emperor, a boy named Romulus Augustulus, was thrown out by a Germanic chief, Odoacer. At that time, Rome had already been plundered twice by Germanic invaders.

During Benedict's youth, Odoacer was overthrown and killed by Theodoric, king of the Germanic Ostrogoths. Theodoric became the new ruler of Italy. So war and insecurity formed the background of Benedict's early life.

City of Vice. After learning to read and write at a local elementary school, Benedict was sent by his parents to study in Rome. At that time, Rome was no longer a center of government. But it was still a great city with magnificent buildings. There were many Christian churches, but there were almost as many pagan temples. According to Gregory, both "Christians and pagans were corrupted with shameful vices."

When Benedict saw how Rome could ruin people, he left. But he stayed long enough to get a good education. His rule shows a wide knowledge of the Fathers of the Church and, of course, the Bible. He was also familiar with great Roman authors such as Virgil, Horace, Livy, and Ovid.

Benedict decided to become a monk. He retreated to a wild, deserted region called Subiaco about 35 miles from Rome. There he found a cave about 1,000 feet above a river gorge. It was lonely enough to warm any hermit's heart. Benedict met a monk who lived in a nearby monastery. This friend gave him a monk's cloak, some religious advice, and a small supply of bread.

Soon, Benedict acquired a group of devoted followers. Although he was young and inexperienced, he organized them into 12 monasteries, each with 12 monks. These monasteries were simply communities of huts. Benedict was hard on himself and disciplined his monks strictly.

After many years, Benedict decided to leave Subiaco and start fresh. With a small group of monks, he traveled south. Finally they stopped at the little town of Cassino. The town was at the foot of a 1,700-foot mountain that is known as Monte Cassino. Benedict climbed the

An eleventh-century manuscript shows St. Benedict writing his rule.

mountain, where there were still some pagan shrines and a temple of Jupiter. On top of the mountain, he and his followers built a small monastery high above the countryside.

Benedict was more than 50 years old when he wrote the rule that would strongly affect the future of monasticism and western Europe. By this time, he was no longer so hard on himself and others. In fact, he had become a calm and moderate man. This is reflected in his rule.

The rule addressed those who wished to live apart from the world and serve God. Early monks, especially in the East, treated their bodies like enemies that had to suffer cold, hunger, and tests of endurance. But Benedict believed that the body should be treated well so that it could better serve the soul.

Daily Routine. To some people at the time, it may have seemed that the monks at Monte Cassino led an easy life. Every day, they spent four hours praying together, four hours praying alone, and about eight hours working. The monks were poor, but they had enough food, clothing, and rest. They slept in quiet dormitories. Each monk had a straw mattress, a rough sheet, a blanket and a pillow.

The monks always ate together. During the winter, they had one meal a day, and two in the summer. This does not seem like a lot today, but to the desert monks of old it would have seemed far too much. All meals were vegetarian, consisting mainly of vegetables, fruit, and grains. Benedict wrote that "a good pound of bread should suffice for the day," and he warned against eating too much. Benedict even allowed his monks to drink some wine. He wasn't happy about this, but he believed that some of the "weaker brethren" needed it. "We read," Benedict said, "that wine is by no means a drink for the monks. But since the monks of our day cannot be per-

Monks cleared the land surrounding the monestaries for crops.

suaded of this, let us at least agree to drink sparingly, 'because wine makes even the wise fall away.' "

Benedict wrote, "He is not a true monk who does not live by the work of his own hands." Benedictine monks worked either within the monastery walls or outside them. They grew enough food and produced enough articles in workshops to sustain their simple life. The monastery was completely self-sufficient and could survive even the worst conditions.

Benedict believed that the better he treated his fellow monks, the more he could require of them spiritually. Instead of putting too great a strain on human nature, he had faith in it. His rule was based on simple virtues—common sense, good judgment, and discretion. He saw himself as the father of a family, one who had to be firm but also just and generous.

The men who followed Benedict's rule at Monte Cassino were from all classes. Many were peasants from the immediate neighborhood, and some were from Germanic tribes. Although many were uneducated to start with, they all learned to read and write. To Benedict, books were important because they could give spiritual guidance. His monks read the Bible and many books by other monks. At Lent each monk was given a book that he was expected to read during that period. The library at Monte Cassino must have been fairly large.

Island of Peace. Benedict wrote his rule at a time when Italy was experienc-

Nuns sometimes lived in convents close to towns. Here, they feed the hungry.

ing the worst suffering in its history. In 535, Justinian, the eastern Roman emperor at Constantinople, sent armies to drive the Germanic tribes out of Italy. The campaign took more than 20 years and brought utter ruin to the country. Famine and disease swept through the land. Survivors did not even bury their dead. In the midst of these horrors, Benedict's monastery offered a haven of peace and security.

Benedict probably remained at Monte Cassino until his death in 547. It is very unlikely that he could have foreseen the far-reaching effects that his rule would have. But in time, Benedictine monasteries would multiply by hundreds and spread throughout the Western world. They would influence the lives of all western Europeans. Benedictine monks built schools and churches, copied books and established libraries. They cultivated farms and forests, and set up infirmaries for the sick and houses for the needy.

Above all, Benedictine monks stressed the ideals of personal worth and serving others. As one historian wrote, "What the haughty Alaric or the fierce Attila had broken to pieces, these patient, meditative men had brought together and made to live again."

✎ Quick Check

1. *What groups preserved culture and Christian teachings through the early Middle Ages? Before Benedict, was there agreement on how to organize the monasteries? How did Benedict change this?*

2. *Why was Benedict sent to Rome? How did he find the life there? Where did he go after leaving Rome?*

3. *What is a monastic rule? How old was Benedict when he wrote his rule? What was special about his rule and his beliefs about people? How were they different from those followed by earlier monks?*

4. *Where did the Benedictines build their monastery after they left Subiaco? Describe how the Benedictines ate and slept. How many hours a day did they pray and work?*

5. *List four ways the Benedictines helped the people outside of their monasteries.*

3
The Legend of King Arthur

What was going on in England while the Merovingians ruled in France? Romans had ruled Britain for centuries. After the fall of Rome in the fifth century, the country was in a state of confusion. Pagan Germanic tribes such as the Saxons and Angles migrated from mainland Europe. They clashed with native British, many of whom had become Christians. These Christians also fought with peoples from northern Britain and Scotland. Many of the northerners were pagan Druids (DREW-ids) who resisted conversion to Christianity. The country was ruled by many minor kings who were constantly at war. Out of all these conflicts rose a question. Who would rule Britain?

No one knows much of what occurred in Britain in the first two centuries after the fall of Rome. Archaeologists have found remains of houses, clothing, pottery, and art. These things indicate how people in that period lived. But there is no way to find out about their government without written records.

Unfortunately, little of what may have been written in that period has survived. Only the records of historians, writers, and poets of later centuries explain anything about Britain in these troubled centuries. Many of them tell the story of Arthur, a great king who united the British people sometime between the sixth and seventh centuries. Many writers told the same story. The most popular version of the story was written by an English writer, Sir Thomas Malory, in the fifteenth century. The following story blends the tales of various writers.

Arthur was the son of Uther Pendragon, king of Britain, and Igraine, the Duchess of Cornwall. Because of a promise his parents made to Merlin the sorcerer, he never really knew his parents. Instead, he was cared for by Ector, a noble lord. Ector raised Arthur as a Christian. Arthur grew up believing that Ector was his father and Ector's son, Kay, was his brother.

The Sword in the Stone. By the time Uther died, the country was in chaos. Arthur was a young man at this point. One day, he and Kay went to a *joust*, which was a lance fight on horseback that men had for fun. On the way to the joust, they passed a huge stone. A gold sword was stuck deep in the stone, and these words were written on it: "Whoever pulls the sword out of the stone shall be king of all England." Many men had tried to pull the sword out of the stone, without success.

When Arthur and Kay arrived at the joust, Kay realized that he had forgotten his sword. Arthur went back to get one.

He ran to the stone and pulled the sword out easily. When Kay saw the

King Arthur (far left) looks on as his knights vow to search for the Holy Grail, a legendary cup used by Jesus.

sword, he bowed to Arthur, hailing him as the new king of England. The knights at the joust also bowed. Then Ector told Arthur that he was not his real father. Arthur was sad, but he promised that as king, he would always help Ector.

Why was the sword so important to the people of England? It was Excalibur, a magic sword that made its wearer victorious in battle. It was made by the Lady of the Lake, a Druid priestess who lived on the mysterious island of Avalon. Avalon was in the center of the sacred lake. No Christian could get to Avalon without the help of one of these priestesses.

As king, Arthur made Kay his steward over all his lands. Then he chose many knights to be his followers. He built a great castle called Camelot. There, he and his knights lived in grace and comfort.

Arthur wanted to get married. Many men wished him to marry their daughters. Arthur chose Guinevere, the lovely daughter of a powerful king. Guinevere's father gave the couple a valuable wedding present—a huge round table that could hold 150 knights. Arthur's knights often feasted and talked while sitting at this table. They became known as the Knights of the Round Table.

Unfortunately, Guinevere fell in love with Arthur's favorite knight. He was Lancelot of the Lake, the son of the Lady of the Lake. Lancelot returned her love. One knight, Sir Meliagaunt, who had secretly loved Guinevere for many years, threatened to ruin the queen's reputation by telling people of her love for Lancelot.

Lancelot challenged him to a duel. It was thought that God would be on the side of the truthful knight. If Lancelot won, Meliagaunt would be proven a liar. If Meliagaunt won, the queen's reputation would be ruined. Lancelot accepted, and both knights mounted their horses and drew their swords. Lancelot killed Meliagaunt and saved the queen's reputation.

Where was Arthur during these problems in his court? He was not home much because he was constantly at war.

Although most of the minor kings of Britain had sworn loyalty to Arthur, some had not. Arthur fought the rebellious kings and brought them under his rule. To preserve order, he let them govern their own lands, but they had to swear loyalty to him.

Arthur also had trouble with his half-sister, Morgan Le Fay. She was a powerful queen and sorceress. She wanted to put her friend, Accolon (ACK-oh-lon), on Arthur's throne. When Arthur and Accolon fought for the throne, Morgan cleverly switched swords. Accolon had Excalibur, but Arthur only had an ordinary sword. Arthur was nearly killed before he discovered the trick. Once he got his sword back, he killed Accolon.

After many years of battle, Arthur subdued the pagan invaders of Britain. Under his rule, many of them abandoned their deities and became Christians. Arthur took much of their wealth as well, which he gave as presents to his best knights. He also conquered much of France. All this added to his wealth and

A medieval knight's armor was so heavy, that the knight had to be lifted onto his horse with a crane.

power. And the people he ruled were united under a Christian king.

Enemies Seize Power. Nevertheless, some of the people in the kingdom were not content. They thought that Arthur spent too much money on wars, making the country poorer. And they grieved for the knights that were killed in battle.

Eventually, Arthur's enemies became more popular with the people of England. The most powerful was Mordred. Mordred wanted to rule England himself.

Mordred waited till Arthur was out of the country. He then showed the English nobles letters which said that Arthur had been killed. Mordred then tried to marry Guinevere. Guinevere pretended to agree to this at first, then ran away. She shut herself up in the Tower of London and surrounded it with soldiers who were loyal to Arthur.

Arthur heard what was happening in his kingdom. He returned with a great navy, intending to kill Mordred and get his throne back. In one-on-one battle, he wounded Mordred fatally. But just as Mordred was dying, he wounded Arthur.

Arthur was badly hurt. He asked one of his knights to take him to the shore of the sacred lake. There, he threw Excalibur into the water. As he lay dying on the shore, a black boat appeared on the lake. The Lady of the Lake and Morgan Le Fay were in it. They helped Arthur into the boat and took him back to Avalon. There he died, and they buried him in a Christian abbey. His most loyal knight, Gawain, became king.

The story of King Arthur meant many things to people of the Middle Ages. These included: order in the midst of chaos, Christian values in the face of paganism, and civilization in the midst of barbaric behavior. Geoffrey of Monmouth (1100-1154) wrote that men and women in Arthur's court were well-dressed, polite, and lived according to the highest ideals of romance.

"The women in Arthur's court scorned to give their love to any man who had not proved himself three times in battle.

In this way the womenfolk became more virtuous, and for their love the knights were ever more daring."

Arthur's knights set an example for medieval warriors in that they followed a code of honor known as *chivalry*. A true knight was not supposed to use his strength against those weaker than himself. He should not scheme to catch an enemy off guard or without a weapon. A fight had to be fair, or there was no honor in winning it. Nor should a true knight pick a fight to show off his strength. He fought only for his lord or his lady. In addition, a *chivalrous* knight had to lead a moral life.

Fact or Fantasy? Did Arthur really exist? Some people believe that he did, and that he is buried in the ruined abbey at Glastonbury, in central England. They think that perhaps he was the last Roman general in Britain, or a Welsh soldier, or a Scottish prince. Others think that the question of whether Arthur existed is less important than what the legend meant to medieval people. The ideal of chivalry set a standard of bravery and manners for all medieval knights. And in a world that often lacked peace, central government, and civilized living, the legend of Arthur's kingdom was a high ideal to reach for.

A king practices falconry, the use of trained hawks for hunting.

✎ Quick Check

1. *Why is so little known about what happened in Britain between the fifth and seventh centuries? Who wrote the most popular version of the legend of King Arthur?*

2. *What was Excalibur? What was its role in choosing the king of England?*

3. *How did King Arthur handle the minor British kings who had not sworn loyalty to him? How did he preserve order among them?*

4. *What caused King Arthur's fall from popularity with his people? Who was Mordred, and how did he gain the throne?*

5. *Define chivalry. Give three examples of what it means. What did the legend of King Arthur mean to people in the Middle Ages?*

4
The Great Emperor

The name "Charlemagne" (SHAR-leh-main) meant Charles the Great, and its owner really looked like a king. He was a big man, more than six feet, four inches tall. He was strong from riding horses, and he could swim faster and better than any of his nobles. He was a kind man when he dealt with his family, friends, and allies. As an enemy, though, he was harsh and unforgiving.

As we have seen, the Frankish kingdoms of Gaul desperately needed a strong leader in the seventh century. The weak Merovingian kings were not interested in nation-building.

In 639, a duke called Pepin seized control and united the kingdoms. A century later, his great grandson, Charlemagne, took over. He reigned from 768 to 814. Under him, the kingdom became the most orderly and unified in Europe since the fall of the Rome.

Charlemagne ruled from the city of Aachen (AHK-un), which he had built as the capital of his kingdom. The city was called a second Rome because the king greatly admired Roman architecture. There were baths, a theater, a forum, and an aqueduct at Aachen, as there were in Rome. Buildings were ornamented with antique columns and mosaics taken from old Roman buildings.

Even more importantly, Charlemagne admired the advanced learning of the Romans. He wanted to educate his people and helped the Church set up schools throughout the kingdom. In them, monks taught boys grammar, arithmetic, geometry, Latin, music, and astronomy. If girls were educated at all, they were taught by nuns or by tutors at home.

However, for all his support of education, Charlemagne himself never learned to write. He kept a writing tablet under

A jewel-adorned likeness of the handsome and proud Charlemagne

Spreading Christianity. The Frankish kingdom at this point was quite large. It included most of France and part of Germany. However, Charlemagne was not content. He wanted to unite all the Germanic tribes into a single Christian state. At this point most Germanic tribespeople were *pagan*. They worshipped many different gods and goddesses. Charlemagne would have to conquer them and make them accept Christianity. His method for doing this was very simple. When he invaded a town, he gave the people a choice between Christianity or death. One afternoon he executed 4,500 people.

Through 53 separate military campaigns, Charlemagne greatly increased the size of his kingdom (see map p. 39). He also forced many tribespeople to become Christians. Converts to Christianity paid taxes to the Franks, whether or not they lived under Charlemagne's rule. Converting pagans to Christianity also increased Charlemagne's standing with the pope at Rome, Adrian I. He depended on Charlemagne to protect Christian interests in Europe.

In 773, Adrian sent Charlemagne a plea for help. The Lombards, a pagan tribe that ruled Italy, were threatening Adrian's life. Charlemagne rode into Rome with a troop of Frankish warriors. He defeated the Lombards and took their king prisoner.

For years, Charlemagne was busy expanding the Frankish kingdom. Five years after he defeated the Lombards, Charlemagne rode into Spain, which was

his pillow so that he could practice before going to bed. When he wanted to write a letter to someone, he dictated it to his personal secretary, a monk named Einhardt (INE-hart). Einhardt also wrote down much of what we know about Charlemagne today.

CHARLEMAGNE'S EMPIRE

MAP EXERCISE

This map shows the growth of the Frankish kingdom under Charlemagne. Use the map to answer the following questions:

1. What river flows near Charlemagne's capital city of Aachen?

2. How far is it from Aachen to Rome?

3. What island in the Mediterranean did Charlemagne conquer?

4. What four peoples were not part of the empire but still paid taxes to Charlemagne?

ruled by Muslims known as *Moors*. The Moors had a more advanced culture than the Franks. This did not matter to Charlemagne. To him, the Moors were barbarians who should be converted to Christianity or thrown out of Spain.

Charlemagne failed to conquer the Moors. While he and his army were retreating through the Pyrenees (PEER-uh-nees) mountains in northern Spain , his army was ambushed. Many soldiers were killed, but Charlemagne survived. This event is remembered in the epic poem *The Song of Roland* (see introduction to Part 1). Some years later, Charlemagne returned to Spain and took over the land as far south as Barcelona.

Charlemagne also made conquests in central and eastern Europe. After 33 years of on-again, off-again battle, he defeated and converted the Saxons of Germany. He also defeated an Asian people called the Avars in what is now Yugoslavia and Hungary. With the Avars gone, Charlemagne freed the native Slavs, who then paid taxes to the Frankish kingdom.

How did Charlemagne govern his new lands? He divided them into counties. Each county was ruled jointly by a bishop and a count. The king regularly sent messengers to his counties to make sure that their rulers obeyed his laws. The laws were a combination of traditional tribal laws and the laws of the

Pope Leo apprehends Charlemagne while praying and crowns him. This picture is from a thirteenth-century encyclopedia.

Catholic Church.

Tribal laws were designed to prevent feuds between families. Every person had a *wergild* (VAIR-gild), or cash value, which was determined by their rank in society. Anyone who injured or killed another was expected to pay a fine based upon the victim's wergild. A murderer had to pay the entire wergild of the victim to his or her family. Then the murder was forgotten.

By 800, Charlemagne controlled the largest empire in Europe since the Roman Empire. Even the pope, Leo III, needed the king. Like his predecessor, Pope Adrian, Leo was threatened by the Lombards. Charlemagne again came to the pope's aid and destroyed the Lombard kingdom once and for all. But Leo's troubles were not over. In Rome, Charlemagne insisted that Leo go on trial. Leo had to swear that he was not guilty of any crimes. That was the only way Leo could get back his power as pope.

Power Plays. Why did Charlemagne shame the pope in this way? Charlemagne said that he, as king, was the ruler of all Christians in western Europe. But Leo said that the pope's power was greater than any king's. The pope, Leo claimed, got his power from God. Leo waited for a time when he could prove this to Charlemagne and European Christians.

On Christmas Day, Charlemagne was praying in St. Peter's Church in Rome. Pope Leo was next to him. Suddenly, Leo took a gold crown from the altar and placed it on Charlemagne's head. The pope said that Charlemagne was now the emperor of western Europe. His empire would be called the Holy Roman Empire.

How did Charlemagne feel about his new title? Some historians claim that he was pleased with it. Others say that he was angry. Charlemagne already ruled western Europe. His new title only provoked his enemies. One thing is certain: Charlemagne did not want Leo to give him the crown. The man who can give a crown can also take it away. Charlemagne did not want the pope to have such power.

Nevertheless, European Christians were happy that the pope had made Charlemagne their emperor. To them, the emperor was a protector blessed by God. Europe would be united again by an emperor and a pope working together.

✎ Quick Check

1. *What was the capital of Charlemagne's kingdom? In what two ways was it like Rome?*

2. *How did Charlemagne "convert" pagans to Christianity? Why did he want to make them Christians?*

3. *Who were the Moors? What happened in Charlemagne's first attempt to conquer them?*

4. *The laws of Charlemagne's lands came from what sources? Explain the importance of a wergild.*

5. *By what act was the Holy Roman Empire created? What did its formation mean to European Christians?*

5
Life on a Manor

Even in Charlemagne's time, a new way of life was taking shape in western Europe. This new way of life was called *feudalism.* It was primarily a way for nobles to obtain military service. Early medieval Europe lacked any central government strong enough to keep order. Therefore, nobles had to rely on their own warriors.

At the top of the feudal system was the nobility. This group was made up of the kings and their lords. Nobles granted land to other nobles in return for their loyalty and military service. A noble who received such land was called a *vassal.* The vassal usually paid taxes to his lord and also provided him with a number of knights (warriors) to help make up an army. In return, he got his land and a promise of protection.

A lord's land was called his *manor.* It was usually worked by poor farmers known as *serfs.* The serfs worked the land and provided food for the manor. In return, they were promised protection from invaders.

Food was a problem for most serfs. Even though they worked ceaselessly, their diet was mainly soup, coarse bread, cheese, and ale. When they had meat, it was usually a small bit used to flavor a stew. Lords and ladies, however, had meat frequently. This was partly because only the lord was allowed to hunt the game on his land. Nobles also had sugar, spices, and dried fruits to flavor their food. Such seasonings were very expensive because they were imported from Africa and Asia.

Most serfs lived in small cottages made of stone or a stick-and-mud mixture called *wattle.* Their roofs were usually covered with straw, and their floors were bare earth. These houses held little besides a rough table, a few stools, and some straw mattresses to sleep on. Serfs were never very comfortable by modern standards.

However, lords and ladies were not much better off. They lived in stone castles that were dark, damp, and drafty. Although they did not have to farm, they had little leisure time. Noble ladies had to supervise servants in the castle, cook, and care for children. They endlessly spun and wove wool for winter clothes and linen for summer clothes. Tasks such as washing clothes, making candles, and butchering were difficult and could take many days. In addition, women of all classes were often exhausted from having too many children. Because so many children died in infancy, it was important to have as many as possible. It was especially important to have sons because daughters usually could not inherit their father's property.

Lords did not have so much day-to-day work. They hunted and helped supervise the serfs. They were not home much, though. Most lords spent a good part of their lives in battle for their king and to protect their manor.

The following conversation is imagined. However, it shows how people lived and thought.

The time: about 850 A.D.

The place: a farm in what is now northern France.

The action: Lord L'Eveque is out riding one afternoon when he comes upon a serf named Henri.

LORD: Well, Henri, I see you have already finished your spring planting. You are a good fellow, Henri. Work hard, and we will all have plenty to eat.

HENRI: Oh, hard work never bothered me, sir. I start working in the fields at dawn and don't stop until sundown. That's not the problem.

LORD: Well, what is the problem?

HENRI: It's all the fighting that goes on, sir. Take last summer, for example. Count Raymond got mad at you because, he said, you were taking fish from his stream. So what did he do? He came over here with several of his knights to get revenge. Well, he couldn't attack your castle. It's too strong. So he set fire to the fields and burned all the crops. Then he killed all the serfs he could find and burned their huts. Now, sir, what's the good of working hard when something like that can happen?

LORD: Yes, you are right about that. It was a great shame. But you see, Henri, that stream really belongs to me. It is on my land, and I can prove it. Don't you worry about that. I will take care of Count Raymond.

HENRI: Well, sir, that's not the only thing that bothers me. It's being tied to this piece of land all my life. The law says that I must stay here and work for you three days a week. My father did it before me, and his father before him. And what do I get in return? You let me have a small part of your land myself. But I can only work on it when I'm not working for you. That gives me just three days, for Heaven forbid that I should work on Sundays. I can't let up for a minute, even in bad weather. It's work, work, work, all the time. On top of that, I have to pay you rent for the land I use. Now is that fair?

LORD: Henri, it is a good thing for you that I am a kind man. Other lords would cut your tongue out for talking like that. The trouble with you, Henri, is that you don't know your place. It is God's will that noblemen be soldiers and that common people serve us.

HENRI: Forgive me, sir, I did not mean to forget my place. It's just that sometimes a man gets very tired.

LORD: Do you think, Henri, that *my* life is easy? I am responsible for law and order here. I must protect my serfs against all enemies. And don't you think that I have a lord and master also? This land doesn't really belong to me. It belongs to *my* lord, the duke. He lets me hold on to it, but in return I must serve him as a soldier. I am sworn to fight for him any time he needs me. But that's not all. I must bring 10 other knights with me. And I have to pay for their horses and armor! That's why you must work for me and pay me rent besides. But it's really not so bad, Henri. On Sundays and holy days, you have plenty of time to enjoy life.

HENRI: Yes, but it's such a short life, sir. Hard work, sickness, and hunger wear a man down. I'll be lucky if I live to be 40.

LORD: What are you complaining about? How many soldiers live that long?

Hearty food is passed around at this celebration of a peasant wedding.

✎ Quick Check

1. *What new way of life was developing in western Europe? Why did nobles need men for military service?*

2. *Define* vassal *and* serf. *How did each serve his lord? What did they get in return?*

3. *What kind of homes did serfs live in? How did noblewomen spend their time? Noblemen?*

4. *Describe a typical work week for Henri the serf. What leisure time did he have? How long did he expect to live? What did people believe was the reason lords and serfs had to serve their separate masters without question?*

45

6
Going to Towns

Not all medieval Europeans lived on manors. By the eleventh century, many had moved to towns. The growth of towns was partly inspired by an extraordinary event—the First Crusade.

In the 1070's, a group of Muslims from central Asia captured Syria and Palestine. They threatened the city of Constantinople (con-stan-tuh-NO-pel), now Istanbul (is-tan-BOOL).

Constantinople was the center of the Byzantine (BIZ-in-teen) Empire. This empire was the successor to the earlier one ruled by Rome. Constantinople was also the seat of the Eastern Orthodox Church. As such, it was a major center of Christian culture. The Byzantine emperor asked Pope Urban II for help in driving the Muslims out of the Holy Land. The emperor expected a small band of paid soldiers. Instead, the pope sent an enormous army of volunteers.

These volunteers were the first *crusaders*. They had many different reasons for joining the Crusades. Many were more interested in capturing territory in the Middle East than helping the Byzantine emperor protect his empire.

The Crusades were also opportunities for Christians to make *pilgrimages*, or journeys to holy places. Usually these places were holy because a saint had lived and performed miracles there. Tours and St. Foy in France were popular places for Christian pilgrims. The crusaders often passed through these places on their way to Jerusalem, the most important holy place.

It was believed that crusaders to Jerusalem received a reward for it in heaven. People also went on the Crusades as penance for their sins. Since the trip was so long and difficult, anyone who returned from Jerusalem was honored.

Crusaders swarm over a medieval city. In the Middle Ages, many wars were fought and lives lost in the name of Christianity.

Lorenzetti's painting of Siena entitled "Effects of Good Government" reveals a certain coziness in the tightly layered life within the walls of a medieval town.

The First Crusade was a success from a military standpoint, and a triumph for the Church. The crusaders helped the Byzantine emperor protect his empire. In addition, they captured Jerusalem and some surrounding areas. Some crusaders stayed and settled in crusader states, lead by Christian rulers.

Inspired by this success, Europeans went on eight more crusades. However, they were unable to gain new territories.

Muslim armies became more powerful. Jerusalem fell to the Turkish Muslims in 1188. Afterwards, the remaining crusader states crumbled.

Towns and Trade. Although the Crusades were military failures, they were economic triumphs. How was this so? The crusaders brought back foreign goods from their journeys. This sparked a demand for trade. Transportation was improving, and travel in Europe was becoming less dangerous. Many people were able to go regularly to markets and trade fairs. Towns soon grew up at these trading centers—towns such as Ghent in northern Europe and Genoa (JEN-uh-wuh) in Italy.

Another reason for the growth of towns in Europe was that farmers were now producing *surplus,* or extra, crops. This meant that not everyone was needed to produce food. So some people became shoemakers or silversmiths. Others specialized in woolen cloth or wine-making. Some areas became famous for one product, and towns developed around the making of that product.

Geography often influenced where new towns would appear. An area near a river, harbor, bridge, or crossroads was a likely place. So was land near a castle or monastery. Such locations were easy to defend.

High Hopes. The same strong faith that sent people on crusades also inspired them to build great churches, or *cathedrals* in many towns. Building a cathedral was expensive and very difficult.

All kinds of people worked on cathe-

Shops selling wares of many kinds lined the streets of medieval towns. This covered market offers shoes, cloth, silver, and gold.

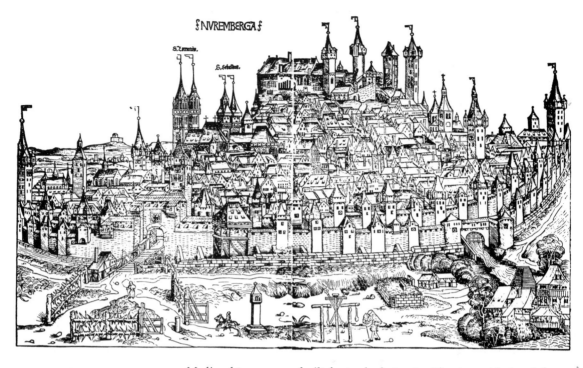

Medieval towns were built for trade, but not without considering defense.
Fifteenth-century Nuremberg, Germany was well guarded by its walls and moat.

drals. Nobles pulled wagons, peasants cut stone blocks. Some of these stone blocks weighed more than a ton. They were brought to the cathedral site in big wagons. People pulled the wagons with long ropes tied around their chests. It took about 150 people, straining with all their might, to pull one wagon.

Why did Christians willingly do the work of animals to build a cathedral? They believed that they would be rewarded in heaven for their work. Also, the results were worth it. Many of the cathedrals built in the Middle Ages were very beautiful. They were the tallest buildings in Europe until modern times. Some were higher than a 30-story build-

ing. To the people of the Middle Ages, these cathedrals seemed to reach toward heaven.

Cathedrals were not only huge, they were beautifully decorated. Most cathedrals had great glass windows of many different colors. These colored windows often showed people and scenes from the Bible. Because most church goers could not read, they learned Bible stories by "reading" the windows. They also admired the paintings, carpets, and statues decorating the cathedrals.

It took about 50 years to build a cathedral, and some took much longer. One reason was that they cost a lot of money. When a town ran out of money, work on the cathedral stopped. Another reason was pride. Each town wanted to build a bigger cathedral than its neighbor. So cathedrals kept getting taller and grander. Some were never finished.

Above all, cathedrals were built to last. One particularly fine example is the cathedral of Chartres, France. It was built three times, beginning in the ninth century. Fire nearly destroyed it four times. The fifth time, the people of Chartres built it to last. It is made of stones carefully balanced on each other to create *Gothic*, or pointed, arches, pillars, and domes.

Construction on the final cathedral began in the twelfth century. Although the basic structure of the building was completed by the fourteenth century, new towers, steeples, and spires were added much later. To this day, the town is proud of its cathedral, and it is carefully maintained. It has survived eight centuries with hardly a scratch.

Freedom in Towns. Many great cathedrals were built in the twelfth and thirteenth centuries. They were a sign that Europe's towns were coming to life. The people also built strong walls around their new towns for protection. Many people won their freedom from feudal lords. Sometimes they paid the lords for the right to govern themselves. Other times they fought for it. Before long, there was a popular saying: "Towns breathe free air." Many serfs ran away to towns to become free.

Medieval towns were busy places, but they were dirty and smelled of garbage.

Usually they had open sewers, and garbage was often thrown in the streets. Diseases were common, and epidemics killed many people. The houses were built mainly of wood and were very close together. If a house caught fire, the whole town might burn down.

But diseases, epidemics, and fires did not stop the towns from growing quickly. Some became overcrowded. Then the old walls were torn down, and larger ones were built so that the town could spread out. Houses were made taller and taller, until, at times, they collapsed.

The people of the towns were proud of their freedom and of their success in business. Many of them wished to thank and honor God for these blessings. The best way they knew was to build a cathedral to God's glory.

✎ Quick Check

1. *Why did Christian volunteers go to the Middle East? What were these volunteers called? Give two reasons why people volunteered.*

2. *How many groups went? Which one, or ones, were successful militarily?*

3. *How did the Crusades contribute to the growth of towns? What other conditions helped towns to grow?*

4. *How long did it take to build a cathedral? Name two reasons why it took so long. What famous cathedral in France was built five times?*

5. *Describe a medieval town. What were some of the hazards of living in one?*

7
The Gentle Servant

Medieval Europe was made up of several social groups. One was those who fought, another those who labored, and a third those who prayed. Not any one of these groups could have existed without the others. All were necessary to the welfare of the whole.

Within the Church there was also a division of labor. Some of the *clergy*, or church people, for example, led very active lives. They traveled to the far corners of Europe trying to convert barbarians. Some even died in the attempt.

Others devoted themselves to trying to imitate the life of Christ. Among religious people, this was perhaps the highest ideal. These people were monks and nuns, and they remained apart from the rest of society. They lived in poverty and gave up all worldly concerns. They owned no property and could not marry. They prayed constantly.

Then there were still others who had something in common with both of these groups. They were the monks who went out and worked among ordinary people. Perhaps the best known of these gentle travelers came from a small town in Italy.

The year: 1207.

The place: the town of Assisi (uh-SIS-ee), Italy.

The action: young Francis di Bernardone (bear-nar-DOE-nay) is on trial as a thief.

A large crowd had gathered in front of the Bishop's palace. The people wanted to see the trial of Francis, who was a rich man's son. Most people in Assisi thought Francis was crazy. Once he was the

For the painter Cimabue, St. Francis was not so much a man as a symbol, an ideal.

town's leading playboy. He and his friends went to parties and drank every night. Then Francis went to war. When he came home, he became very sick and was near death for several weeks. Finally he got well again.

But Francis had changed. He did not care about parties and drinking anymore. He began giving all his money away to beggars. And he took care of people who were shut up in special hospitals with an ugly disease called leprosy. Francis's father, Peter, became very angry with him. He wanted Francis to work in his shop and sell cloth. Why was Francis wasting time and money helping useless people? Peter thought his son was crazy.

One day Francis was praying in an old, rundown church. He believed he heard a voice that said, "Francis, repair my church." Francis was sure that God had spoken to him. He wanted very much to serve God and do God's work, but he would need money to fix the church. Where would he get it? Then he thought of the fine cloth in his father's store. He took some of it and sold it.

Francis's father soon found out what he had done. Peter became red with anger and called his son a thief. He de-

Giotto's painting of Saint Clare weeping over the body of Saint Francis

manded that Francis be put on trial for stealing. He wanted to punish Francis and get back the money for his cloth.

The judge in the trial was the bishop of Assisi. He liked Francis and knew that he wanted to serve God. "But," he said, "you have no right to keep money that you got by stealing. You must give it back to your father."

"I will not only give him the money," Francis said, "I will do more." Then Francis went inside the bishop's palace. He came out a few minutes later, completely naked. He was holding his clothes in his hands. Then he shouted to the crowd:

"Up to now, I have called Peter my father. But now I plan to serve God. I am returning to Peter his money and all the clothes I got from him. From now on I shall call God, not Peter, my Father."

Francis threw his purse and his clothes at Peter's feet. Then the bishop covered Francis with his own coat. Many people in the crowd felt sorry for Francis and cried. He had given up his home and family forever. But Francis went away singing. He would find his joy in life doing God's work.

A New Order. Francis later started an *order* (group) of monks that thousands of men joined. These monks had to live, like Francis, in complete poverty. They could own only the simple clothes they wore. Their homes were huts, and they slept on the ground. They had to work for their food, or beg for it.

Earlier monks had lived in remote areas of the countryside. Franciscan monks lived and worked in Europe's growing towns. The people of the towns sometimes seemed to forget God in their rush for wealth and power. The Franciscans reminded townspeople that they must serve God too.

Francis's monks were so successful that in 1212 he founded an order for women headed by Clare of Assisi. She was a noble lady who escaped an arranged marriage by taking refuge in a nunnery. There, she met Francis and adopted his ideals. Her order attracted many women from all social classes. Clare was credited with saving Assisi from invaders at least twice. On the first occasion, she greeted the invaders by offering them the Holy Sacrament. Confused, the invaders retreated.

Francis's followers spent their lives helping the poor and the sick. When Francis died, he was declared a saint of the Church. Clare was made a saint as well. Franciscan monks and nuns still carry on their work today.

✎ Quick Check

1. *What were three of the social groups that made up medieval Europe? What were two groups within the Church?*

2. *What was Francis like before he went to war? Why was he put on trial? What order did he start?*

3. *Before Francis's time, how did monks live and work? How did Francis's order change this?*

4. *Who was Clare of Assisi, and what did she do?*

8
Eleanor of Aquitaine

Lady, I'm yours and yours shall be
Vowed to your service constantly,
This is the oath of loyalty
I pledged to you this long time past
As my first joy was all in you,
So shall my last be found there too,
So long as life in me shall last.

Bernart de Ventadour

A queen named Eleanor of Aquitaine (ACK-wih-tane) requested this verse in the twelfth century. Eleanor wanted to create a new society, where women were worshipped as goddesses by brave and civilized knights. She wanted to teach men and women to love each other in a refined and civilized way. Eleanor believed that refined, or *courtly* love would protect women in an unfair world.

Why? Even as a queen, Eleanor was often treated as her husband's property. In fact, medieval government and the Church made this treatment law. A smart and spirited woman, Eleanor challenged the Church and her two husbands, King Louis VII of France and King Henry II of England.

She was the daughter of Duke William of Aquitaine. He ruled much of central and southwestern France. The Romans named it Aquitaine, which means "land of the waters," because four rivers crisscross it. The duke also ruled Poitou (pwah-TOO), a small county north of Aquitaine.

A Well-rounded Education. Eleanor, born in 1122, was brought up in a court filled with poet-musicians called *trouba-*

These two figures, representing a king and queen of Judah, were modeled after Eleanor of Aquitaine and Louis.

dours. They sang songs of love and romance. Eleanor learned their songs, but she also learned more serious things. She was one of the few women of her age to get a good education. She could read and speak Latin and Provencal (pro-ven-SAHL), as well as the *langue doc,* her native language. She learned arithmetic and what was known of astronomy. In her free time, she enjoyed riding horses and hunting with falcons.

Eleanor's father died when she was 15. He left Aquitaine and Poitou to her, because he had no sons. Fortune-hunting knights from all over France plotted to kidnap Eleanor and force her to marry them. The man she married could take control of her land.

Louis VI, also called Louis the Fat, was the king of France. In theory he ruled all of France. But his actual kingdom was much smaller than Eleanor's. King Louis decided Eleanor should marry his 16-year-old son, Louis VII. Then Aquitaine would be united to his own kingdom, which was centered in Paris.

Eleanor at first was glad to be marrying a prince. She and Louis VII were married in 1137. Shortly after the wedding, news came that Louis VI had died from overeating. Eleanor was now queen of France. She and Louis went to live in the royal palace in Paris.

The marriage was a great disappointment to both. Louis was very religious. He was far more like a monk than a noble knight. He loved Eleanor but could not understand her love of pleasure. She tried to make the gloomy royal palace into a gay court like that she had left in Aquitaine. She was annoyed because Louis did not let her govern equally with him. Both were unhappy because Eleanor did not have a son to inherit the throne. Instead, she had two daughters.

Adventure to the East. Eleanor abandoned her dull life in 1147. Against the protests of Louis, she insisted on accompanying him on the Second Crusade to Jerusalem, the Holy Land. The Turks were threatening to invade and make Jerusalem part of Muslim territory.

Accompanied by noblewomen, maids, and troubadours, Eleanor joined the crusade. It was a complete disaster. Even before they reached Jerusalem, a large part of the army was ambushed by the Turks and suffered terrible losses.

For Eleanor, though, the Second Crusade was not a total loss. She was awed by the splendor of cities like Constantinople and Antioch (AN-tee-ock) in the East. There, Greek and Roman learning and living standards still endured.

At Antioch, Eleanor met her uncle, Prince Raymond. He turned out to be her ideal of a brave and charming knight. Unfortunately, Louis was jealous of their friendship. He insisted that she leave Antioch and continue to Jerusalem. She refused, because she thought that it made little military sense to leave a safe city at that time. Also, she was happier in Antioch than she had ever been in Paris. Finally, she made a formal statement to Louis that she wanted to leave him and remain in Antioch.

Louis was stubborn. He still loved Eleanor and did not want to lose the rich lands of Aquitaine and Poitou. One night, he kidnapped her and dragged her to Jerusalem. Eleanor raged over her own helplessness. This no doubt strengthened her decision to leave Louis.

Back in France, Eleanor demanded that the Church set aside her marriage. She claimed that Louis and she were blood relations (actually, they were fourth cousins). Louis had his own reasons for agreeing to the annullment. He wanted a male heir and hoped that another wife could give him one.

Eleanor had already decided to marry a prince, Henry Plantagenet of Anjou. He was young, handsome, and heir to the throne of England. Although Eleanor, at 29, was 11 years his senior, she was beautiful, intelligent, cultured, and ruled a kingdom much bigger than his own. She proposed to him, and he immediately accepted.

Eight weeks after her first marriage ended, Eleanor married Henry. The king of England soon died, and Henry became king. He founded what is now known as the Angevin (AN-jeh-vin) kingdom. It included England and parts of France (see map p. 59).

Eleanor and Henry had five sons and three daughters in 13 years. Among them were the future English kings Richard the Lionhearted and John. However,

THE ANGEVIN KINGDOM

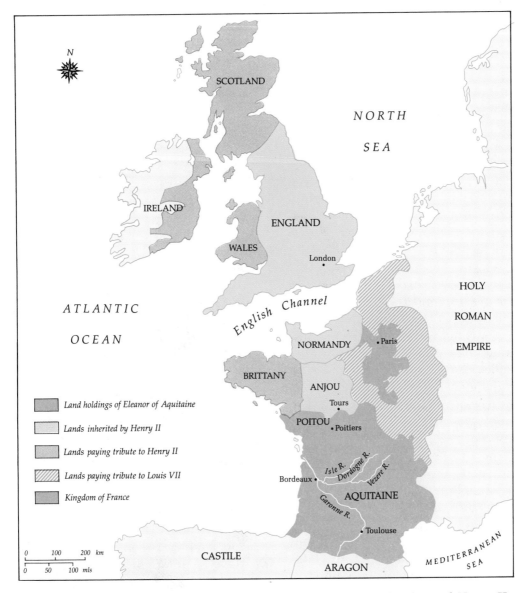

This map shows the land holdings of Eleanor of Aquitaine, Louis VII, and Henry II at the end of the twelfth century. Use the map to answer the following questions.

1. Name three lands that Henry II inherited? What land did he gain by marrying Eleanor?

2. What land lay directly to the south of Aquitaine? What empire lay east of Paris?

3. Which kingdom was larger, the kingdom of France or the Angevin kingdom?

4. The Romans named Eleanor's land Aquitaine because four rivers crisscross it. Name two of them.

Henry was even less inclined than Louis to share his power with Eleanor. He even insisted on ruling Aquitaine himself. She was allowed to carry out his instructions when he was out of the country. But that was all, and it made her angry.

To be fair, Henry was not a bad king. He tried to be just. One of his most important deeds was to introduce the system of trial by jury, which replaced the system of trial by ordeal (see p. 25).

After Eleanor had borne her last child, John, Henry fell deeply in love with a beautiful noblewoman, Rosamond Clifford. This was more than Eleanor could bear. In 1167, she told Henry that she was leaving him and returning to Aquitaine. Her fourth son and favorite child, Richard, was her heir, and she wanted to teach him to govern her land.

The Ideal Court. In Aquitaine Eleanor set up the ideal court of her dreams. In Poitiers (pwah-tee-AY), her father's palace came alive once again. Troubadours, scholars, and writers flocked to Eleanor's court. She and her first daughter, Marie of Champagne, enjoyed the troubadours' flowery compliments and love poetry.

Eleanor and Marie created a fantasy world where women ruled supreme and men existed only to worship them. They recorded their ideals and beliefs in a book called *The Code of Love*. It contained 31 rules for men to obey when dealing with women. Among these rules were the following:

• You must be obedient to the commands of women.

• You must in all things be polite and courteous.

• You must be faithful to her whom you love.

Meanwhile, Eleanor's three oldest sons—Henry, Richard, and Geoffrey—became worried about their future. King Henry threatened to take part of their inherited lands and give them to John, his last and favorite son. In 1173, the three

Eleanor's tomb (top). The lion and unicorn on either side of the woman in the tapestry (bottom) symbolize chivalry.

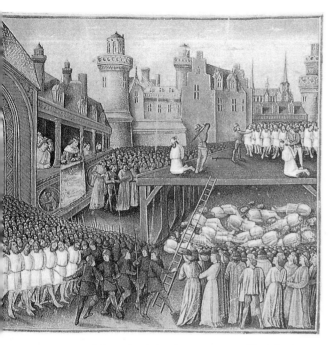

Many brutal acts were committed during the Crusades. Here, King Richard I (middle, left) looks on as prisoners are executed.

Throughout his 10-year reign, Richard spent most of his time on the Crusades to the Holy Land. Eleanor ruled in his place. She finally proved her ability to govern, and govern well.

Some of Eleanor's work survives to this day. Modern manners mirror her ideals of courtly romance. For example, the ideas that "ladies always go first" and that a man should open a door for a woman come from the court of Poitiers. However, her deeds went beyond encouraging courtesy. At a French abbey, she founded a shelter for battered noblewomen. When she ruled England, she pardoned prisoners whom she thought had been punished enough. Always she tried to encourage justice and generosity. Most scholars consider her the most extraordinary woman of the Middle Ages.

✎ Quick Check

1. *When was Eleanor of Aquitaine born? Where was Aquitaine, and how did it get its name? Describe Eleanor's early education.*

2. *What sort of treatment did Eleanor fight against?*

3. *Who was Eleanor's first husband? Where did they travel and why? Give two reasons for the end of their marriage.*

4. *Who was Eleanor's second husband? What kingdom did he rule? Of what two countries was Eleanor queen in her lifetime?*

5. *What was Eleanor's opinion of marriage? List three of the codes of love set up by Eleanor in Aquitaine. What were her other important achievements?*

revolted against Henry. Eleanor and her ex-husband King Louis supported them. Henry put down the rebels and made peace with his sons. But he was not ready to forgive Eleanor. A few months later, he took her prisoner and locked her in a dreary castle in England.

For the next 16 years, until Henry's death, Eleanor was kept under house arrest. She learned as much as she could about politics from her guards, most of whom were nobles. After Henry died, she had a great deal of influence over the Angevin kingdom. Her favorite son, Richard, became king of England.

PART 1
Review and Skills Exercises

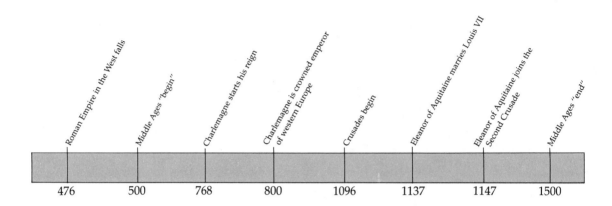

Roman Empire in the West falls | Middle Ages "begin" | Charlemagne starts his reign | Charlemagne is crowned emperor of western Europe | Crusades begin | Eleanor of Aquitaine marries Louis VII | Eleanor of Aquitaine joins the Second Crusade | Middle Ages "end"

476   500   768   800   1096   1137   1147   1500

Understanding Events

In Part 1, you read of some of the dramatic events that took place in western Europe during the period known as the Middle Ages. This long period was marked by shifting borders, the development of feudal society, and the spread of Christianity. The time line above gives some important events of the period. Study the time line and answer the questions.

1. Approximately when did the Middle Ages begin? About when did the period end? How many years did it last?

2. When did Charlemagne begin ruling? How many years after that was he crowned emperor?

3. Which event occurred first: Eleanor of Aquitaine marries Louis VII or Eleanor of Aquitaine joins the Second Crusade?

4. How many years passed between the end of the Roman Empire in the west and the beginning of the Crusades?

5. Who lived first, Charlemagne or Louis VII?

Relating Geography to History

You read in Chapter 6 how geography influenced the growth of towns in the Middle Ages. Geography also influenced the growth of trade. In the passage below you will read how some noblemen in France used the location of their lands to increase trade. The passage is adapted from *A History of the Middle Ages, 284–1500*, by Sidney Painter. Read the passage and answer the questions that follow.

Early in the twelfth century the counts of Champagne (sham-PANE), a key region in northeastern France, saw a way to make money. They held lands between the Saône River and tributaries of the Rhine, Seine, and Loire rivers. The valleys of these rivers were good overland travel routes.

The counts set to work to turn their lands into a vast market place. At a number of chief towns they founded fairs. The counts set aside places for the fairs, erected booths, provided police to keep order, and judges to settle disputes. They also set up money-changers to handle the wide variety of coins brought in by merchants from many lands. The counts collected a sales tax on all goods sold at the fair, rented the booths at good prices, and received the money penalties paid for offenses against the rules of the fair. The barons who lived along the chief routes by which merchants traveled to the fairs were offered annual payments. In return for the payments, the barons were to protect the merchants.

The fairs of Champagne became the meeting place of the merchants from Italy and those of the north. The Italians brought products of Italy such as cloth, fine swords, and magnificent Lombard war horses. They also brought the silks, sugar, and spices they had obtained in Syria. The men of the far north brought furs, honey, and other products of the great forests. From Flanders (part of modern-day Belgium) came cloth, and from England, tin.

The great fairs were essentially what we call wholesale markets. Foreign merchants would bring their goods and sell them to local merchants who would distribute them throughout the country. For about two hundred years the fairs of Champagne were the most important market places in western Europe.

1. On a map of modern Europe find France, Italy, England, and Belgium. Then find the Rhine, Seine, and Loire rivers. Explain why the area of northeastern France near these rivers was a good meeting place for merchants from countries in Europe.

2. In general, why are river valleys good travel routes?

3. How do you think the Champagne fairs helped to encourage trade?

4. What costs did the counts have in setting up the fairs? How did the counts make money from the fairs?

5. What information in the passage tells that Italians traded outside of Europe?

Building Vocabulary

Below are 10 words from the passage on the fairs of Champagne. Reread the passage to review the use of each word. Then choose eight of the words. On a sheet of paper, use each word in a separate sentence. Refer to a dictionary if you are unsure of the meaning of a word.

tributaries	magnificent
disputes	invaluable
penalties	essentially
offenses	wholesaler
annual	distribute

PART

2

THE RISE OF NATIONS

During the spring of 1066, a call for good shipbuilders went out in northern France. On the beaches of Normandy, men hired by Duke William were building ships as fast as they could. Woodcutters were chopping down trees for masts and rudders. Weavers were making sails.

William, Duke of Normandy, wanted to be king of England. He said that he had been promised the throne by the former English king. And so, to unseat the present king, Harold, William was going to invade England. It was a daring and dangerous move.

By June, builders were pushing William's ships into the water. They no sooner finished one ship than they started on the next. Some ships were striped in bright colors from stem to stern. Others were painted black, like the ships of Viking sailors from Scandinavia. It was not surprising that some Norman ships should look like those of the Vikings. For the Normans were descendants of Vikings who had settled in northern France.

The fleet was ready by the end of June. William had 500 large ships and many smaller ones. Soldiers began loading the ships with armor, swords, and wooden crossbows. At the last moment, they led their horses on board. They knew that a battle lay ahead. Their horses might help them win it.

The fleet waited all summer for the right wind. Finally, in September, it set sail. The next morning the Normans saw the coast of England. Quietly, their boats inched toward shore and slid onto the beach. William jumped from his boat and dropped to the ground. "Look," he cried, "I have seized England with both hands!"

The Battle of Hastings. At the time of William's landing, King Harold was in northern England. When he learned of the invasion, he marched his troops 240 miles to meet William. On October 14, 1066, the two armies met at Hastings, a town near the southern coast. There were about 7,000 to 8,000 men on each side.

At first King Harold had an advantage over William. He placed his men on the top of a hill and ordered them not to move. Some of the Normans fled. Harold's men ran in pursuit, breaking ranks. That opened a hole for William's horsemen to enter. King Harold was killed in the fighting. His army lost heart and began to run away. In the end, William's forces won the Battle of Hastings.

William, thereafter known as William the Conqueror, became king of England. He was crowned on Christmas Day, 1066. Many of Harold's followers left the country. William's men took their land. Now Norman knights and lords became the rulers of England.

Normans recorded their conquest of England on a 200-foot Bayeux tapestry. Page 64: Court of France's Charles VII, one of the first national assemblies.

Two Peoples Become One. Despite their differences, the Normans and the English shared one bond. That was religion. Both groups thought of themselves as Christians. Most Christians felt that they had a duty to support a rightful leader. William insisted that the defeated English owed their loyalty to him. In return, William was careful not to change English laws or the English form of government. The English finally accepted him and his descendants as rightful kings.

Language was a greater problem. At first the Normans and the English could not understand one another. The Normans spoke French; most of the English spoke Anglo-Saxon. But little by little, each learned some of the other group's language. In time, the two groups spoke a mixture of French and Anglo-Saxon. The English that we speak today is based on this mixture of French and Anglo-Saxon.

Normans and English also grew closer in other ways. For example, more and more Normans and English married each other. The children of these marriages had the blood of both groups in their veins.

In the end, the Normans and the English became one people. At about the same time, other groups were developing similar bonds in other parts of Europe. These bonds were of several kinds: language, religion, leadership. In each case, they helped to create the nations we know today.

9
The Great Charter

John "Lackland" was the youngest of the five sons of England's King Henry II and Eleanor of Aquitaine. No one could have expected that John would ever be king of England. Even his nickname, Lackland, hinted at misfortune. His father, Henry II, had no land to give his youngest son when John was born.

John became king purely by chance. Three of his brothers died before their father did. The fourth brother became King Richard I in 1189. This brother was called Richard the Lionhearted because of his bravery in battle. Yet Richard's acts of daring were costly for his subjects.

Overtaxing. First, English taxpayers gave Richard a great sum of money to go on a crusade. Then, on his way back from the crusade, Richard was captured and held for ransom. To free him, the English again had to pay a large sum.

Once Richard reached England, he planned another adventure. This time it was war with the king of France. The English groaned as Richard's men collected still more in taxes.

In 1199 Richard was wounded in battle. The wound failed to heal, and Richard died. John inherited the crown of England. But along with the crown came a huge pile of debts.

It was up to John to pay these debts. As king of England, he had many ways to collect money. All landowners had to pay him a fee. He could buy goods at low prices and sell them at higher prices than he paid. The English people had to help him build his castles. They had to lend him horses and carts when necessary. John himself was the judge of when such things were needed.

John tried to save money by cutting

The Great Seal of King John used to "sign" the Magna Charta

back on services. He ended the practice of sending the king's judges out to settle quarrels. Now people had no one to settle disputes.

Feud with the Church. John's way of handling money was not popular with England's feudal lords. He also had a long and bitter quarrel with Pope Innocent III. The quarrel centered on the naming of a man to be archbishop of Canterbury. This archbishop was to be one of the two leaders of the Church of England.

According to tradition, Canterbury monks were supposed to choose the archbishop. In fact, however, the choice was usually made by the king. In 1205 the monks chose one archbishop and King John chose another. The pope then stepped into the dispute by naming a third.

But King John refused to allow the pope's man, Stephen Langton, to enter England. He also ordered the Canterbury monks out of the country. And so the pope issued an order called an *interdict*. Under the interdict, no one in England could marry or be baptized or buried with a proper Church service. The interdict made John even angrier. He seized Church lands in the name of the crown.

After seven years John made his peace with the pope. Stephen Langton was admitted to England. But by this time John had come to seem cruel and crafty. England's lords were uneasy. They had begun to think of themselves as national spokesmen. Now they wondered what they could do to protect themselves against the king.

Challenging the King. The answer was supplied by Langton. He had become John's main opponent. He now pointed to a *charter*, or contract, that John's great-grandfather, Henry I, had signed when he became king in 1100. In this charter, the king had promised certain liberties to the clergy and lords. "Why," Stephen asked, "can't John do the same?"

The lords seized on this idea. They would write a new charter. The charter would make clear what responsibilities the king had to the lords, and what the lords in turn owed to the people under them. The lords would make the king sign it. Then, if John did not keep his promises, they could get rid of him.

John himself gave them their chance to

strike. He led an army to attack France. While in France, he sent home an order for more taxes. The lords delayed payment. Because of difficulties in France, John lost the war. He came back to England defeated and in need of money.

Now the lords saw their chance. A large group of them told John that they would not pay his taxes. They would rebel unless he agreed to their demands. They fortified their castles and prepared for war.

John did not want to limit his own power. But he saw that England would be thrown into turmoil if he did not give in. So he agreed. In 1215 he met the lords in a meadow called Runnymede, 20 miles up the Thames (temz) River from London.

A King Must Bow. At Runnymede the lords presented the king with a document stating their demands. This was the Magna Charta (MAG-nuh CART-uh), a Latin term meaning "great charter." The king put his seal to it. Within a week, both sides had put the finishing touches to the Magna Charta.

The Magna Charta strongly curbed the king's power. John was not to limit the freedom of the Church. He was not to tax land without a meeting of the leading landowners, the lords. In selecting his officials, John was to choose only those "who know the law of the realm and mean to observe it well." Again and again, the stress was put on the law.

Another part of the charter was a promise to people called "free men."

These were the lords and some common people as well. The king could not put any free man in prison without a trial. That meant that the king had to have a good reason for jailing a free man. He could not simply lock up a troublemaker, as John had done in the past.

John agreed to all the terms of the Magna Charta. But the agreement did not end his conflict with the lords. The disputes continued until October 1216, when John suddenly died. But the Magna Charta lived on after him.

If anything, the charter mostly preserved the rights lords already thought they held. It certainly did not bring any radical changes. Still, the Magna Charta had an importance the English people never forgot. It said that even a king must bow when the people are sure of their rights. The king himself must be ruled by law.

In 1295, another event helped to shape the way the English made their laws. It was 80 years after the signing of the Magna Charta. The current king, Edward I, decided to call a meeting of his council. It was made up of the clergy and nobles appointed by the king. But Edward wanted to enlarge the meeting. He ordered that elections be held throughout England. Free men were to choose *representatives* to attend. The representatives would speak for those who voted. This meeting became known as the Model Parliament. It was a *model*, or example, for all such meetings that followed.

The Model Parliament was the first

Figure of King John on his tomb in Worcester Cathedral in England.

with elected representatives called by a king. In time, Parliament would break into two groups. The nobility would form one body, called the House of Lords. The knights and citizens would form another, called the House of Commons.

In the long run, the Magna Charta and the rise of Parliament helped to limit the power of the English crown. Both helped make England a land ruled by laws instead of individuals. In doing so, these two events built a sense of unity among the English people. And that unity helped make England a strong nation.

✎ Quick Check

1. *In twelfth-century England, how did the king get money from the people?*

2. *What was John's quarrel with the Church? What did John do? How did the Church respond?*

3. *Who was Stephen Langton? What did he do to limit the power of the king? Who liked his ideas? Why?*

4. *What does* Magna Charta *mean? When was it signed? How did it curb the king's power? What did it promise to "free men"?*

5. *What was the Model Parliament? How was it different from the council meetings before? How did it help unify England?*

10
The Maid of Lorraine

Legends of chivalry became popular in France in the late Middle Ages. One of them predicted that France would be saved by a maiden. She would come from an oak forest and would dress in a man's clothes.

At some points in French history, this story might have been shrugged off as silly. In 1429, however, it had great meaning. People believed that the legend had come true. It looked as though a teenaged girl might save France.

France had been waging an on-again, off-again war with England since 1337. This conflict was started by the English. King Edward III claimed the French crown to protect his land in France. The struggle was later known as the Hundred Years' War.

By 1429 the French needed to be saved.

The English held all of France north of the Loire (lwahr) River. Furthermore, King Charles VI of France had died in 1422. He left his crown to the English king, not to his son, the *dauphin* (doe-FAN) Charles. (*Dauphin* means the eldest son of a French king.)

In May 1428, a girl of 16 walked into a French stronghold named Vaucouleurs (vow-coo-LUHR). She asked to see the captain. She told him that God had sent her. She asked the captain to write the dauphin and say, "Joan will lead you to your crowning."

The French captain listened politely. The girl's story seemed fantastic, even in an age of religious faith. So the captain sent the girl home to her village. But that was not the end of Jeannette, or Joan of Arc, as she was later called.

Joan's Visions. Joan came from the gentle, rolling countryside of eastern France. Near her village in the region of Lorraine (luh-RAIN) rose a dark forest called the Wood of Oaks. One day in her father's garden a great light burst forth, or so she later claimed. She believed that the Archangel Michael had appeared to her. He urged her to have greater faith.

Joan followed this advice. She kept hearing voices and seeing visions. Finally, the Archangel Michael appeared again. He told her to go to the aid of her king. There was no French king at the time. So Joan chose to aid the French dauphin.

A few months after Joan's first trip to Vaucouleurs, English forces laid siege to Orleans (or-lay-AHN). This city on the Loire River was critical. If it fell to the English, the French would probably lose the war. But as long as the French held the city, a glimmer of hope remained.

At this important moment, Joan went back to Vaucouleurs. In January 1429, the captain gave in to her wish to see the dauphin. Joan and a few friends arrived at the royal palace at Chinon (she-NON) in March. Soon after their arrival, members of the clergy questioned Joan. She told them that she had two goals. The first was to lift the siege of Orleans. The second was to see the crowning of the dauphin as king of France.

The clergy must have been astonished. Some of them may have noticed the differences between Joan and the dauphin Charles. Joan was healthy, strong, and good-looking, with an open, smiling face. Charles was sickly, homely, and afraid for his life.

The dauphin agreed to see Joan. She was shown to a room where he and his court were gathered. There was no way for Joan to tell which of these people was the dauphin. Yet legend has it that Joan picked Charles out of the group. "Most noble prince," she said, "I have come from God to help you and your kingdom." Joan later claimed that her voices had guided her to the dauphin.

Leading France to Victory. Charles decided to let Joan have her way. He had her fitted for a suit of armor. He chose one of his most powerful dukes to help her assemble an army. Joan gave the French hope. They were not afraid to volunteer in her service. By the last week of April, her army numbered between 3,000 and 4,000 men.

On April 29, Joan and her troops sneaked past the English and entered Orleans. Until their arrival, the city's mood had been close to despair. The English siege had been going on for several months. There seemed no way to lift it. Now Joan's clear, direct leadership sparked enthusiasm. Many of the townspeople believed she had indeed been sent by God.

First Joan asked the English to surrender. They laughed at the idea of surren-

Eventually, Joan of Arc was cleared of her "sins" and canonized, made a saint, centuries later.

dering to a woman. So Joan and her troops met the English in several battles. The most important one was on May 7. Joan was wounded in the shoulder by an arrow. But the English were defeated and driven from the city's gates. Soon the French took several other towns as well.

Joan had succeeded in the first of her two goals. Fresh from victory, she became impatient to win the second. She told the dauphin that the time was right for his crowning. As king, Charles would get more respect from his subjects.

Crowning the King. By custom, French kings were crowned in a majestic cathedral in the northern town of Reims (reemz). To get there, the king's party would have to travel through enemy territory. Joan and the army led the way. They won several military victories along the route. On July 16, the dauphin became King Charles VII. Joan stood at his side, her banner in her hand. "Gentle king," she said, "the will of God is now fulfilled."

Once Charles became king, he showed a will of his own. Joan wanted him to drive the enemy from Paris. But Charles refused. Joan, meanwhile, began to feel that she did not have long to live. Impatient to complete her mission, she went to Paris herself. While fighting in a nearby town in May 1430, she was captured by the enemy.

They could have killed her on the spot. Instead they decided to make use of her. Though Joan had been fighting only a year, she had become important to the French. The English wanted to weaken French faith in her.

They moved Joan from castle to castle. Finally, they imprisoned her in the town of Rouen (roo-AHN) near the coast. They left her in the hands of a French bishop who was bitterly opposed to Charles VII. The bishop assembled a Church court which held views similar to his.

Trial at Rouen. From February to May 1431, Joan was questioned and heckled and threatened. She was told that she could not claim she knew God's will better than the clergy did. She was called a sinner. Her captors would not allow her to attend mass unless she wore women's clothes. But Joan stubbornly refused to back down. She would not wear wom-

MAP EXERCISE

This map shows how France was divided in 1429 during the Hundred Years' War. Use the map to answer the following questions.

1. On what river is Rouen located?

2. What two rivers come together near the town of Bordeaux?

3. How far is Vaucouleurs from Orleans?

4. What body of water separates England from the territory it controlled in France?

FRANCE IN 1429

ENGLAND

London

Calais

ENGLISH CHANNEL

Cherbourg

Rouen

Seine River

Oise River

Paris

Reims

Marne River

Vaucouleurs

Domrémy

Schelde River

Meuse River

Rhine River

Moselle River

LORRAINE

Orleans

Loire River

Chinon

BURGUNDY

Loire River

Saône River

F R A N C E

ATLANTIC

OCEAN

Bordeaux

Dordogne River

Garonne River

Rhône River

SAVOY

PROVENCE

SPAIN

MEDITERRANEAN SEA

N
W E
S

■ Territory Loyal to King Charles VII

■ Territory Held by England and Burgundy

Scale of Miles

0   25   50   100   150

en's clothes because she wanted to be treated as a warrior. She would not renounce her voices, for that would be a lie.

It soon became clear that Joan was to be burned at the stake as a witch. After several months of torment, she wavered in her thinking. She gave in to the Church court. She even put on women's clothes. But her change of heart lasted only a few days. Finally, she informed her judge that she was sorry that she had given in. Now she was ready to die for her beliefs.

On May 30, 1431, Joan was taken to the old market square in Rouen. She was chained to a stake in the middle of some firewood. A torch was put to the wood. A wisp of smoke rose, then the smoke turned to flame. Joan cried out, "Jesus!" Within a few minutes, she was dead.

Joan of Arc is tied to the stake before an audience of her persecutors.

King Charles had not lifted a finger to save her.

Joan became a folk heroine to the French. Yet her victories did not end the Hundred Years' War. In 1436 Charles VII won by treaty what Joan had not won in battle—the city of Paris. Still, the war dragged on.

It did not come to an end until 1453. In that year the French drove the English from the coastal city of Bordeaux (bore-DOE). Now the English were left with only one last foothold on French soil. This was the port city of Calais (kah-LAY).

The war broke the ties between France and England. Back in 1337, the English had been near-relatives to the French. Now England began to think of itself as England. France came to think of itself as France.

✎ Quick Check

1. *What was the Hundred Years' War? When did it begin?*

2. *What was unusual about Joan of Arc? What conditions in France at that time explain her popularity? When did she first offer her services? How old was she?*

3. *Who was the dauphin? To what two missions of Joan's did he agree? How did Joan complete each mission?*

4. *How did the English make use of Joan after her capture? What was her trial like? What was the verdict?*

5. *How and when did the Hundred Years' War end? What happened to the ties between France and England?*

11
Conquests in Spain

After the fall of Rome, people in Spain eagerly embraced Christianity. But in 711 Spain was invaded by a Muslim people from North Africa. These were the Moors. They ruled much of Spain for the next seven centuries.

Why were the Moors able to take over Spain? The Spanish people were not united. Many did not even speak the same language. The ruling class were Visigoths, a Germanic tribe that had converted to Christianity. They kept themselves carefully apart from native Spanish Christians and Spanish Jews. In 711, a Visigoth ruler asked a Moorish general, Tariq (TAH-rik), to aid him against another Visigoth leader. After Tariq ended the quarrel, he stayed in Spain and fought against the Visigoths. Most native Spaniards preferred their new conquerors to the Visigoths.

Moors Bring Improvements. However, that did not mean that they really liked their new rulers. Most Christians in Spain were quick to dismiss their conquerors as barbarians. Actually, the Moors were extremely civilized. Their trade brought foreign luxuries to Spanish ports. Moorish artists and architects built elegant palaces and *mosques*, or Muslim temples. Moorish doctors recognized many diseases and knew how to treat them. They could cure cataracts in the eye, heal wounds, give antidotes for poisons, and remove cancerous tumors.

The Moors set up universities in the cities of Granada (gruh-NAHD-uh), Seville (suh-VEEL), and Cordoba (CORD-oh-vuh). They became important learning centers in Europe. In them, students could study algebra, which the Moors invented. They also could learn philosophy, medicine, poetry, Greek, and astronomy. Under the Moors, Spaniards became some of the best-educated people in Europe.

Moorish improvements did not stop with education and trade. In the cities, people walked along lighted streets at night. Unlike most western Europeans, the Moors believed in bathing often. They built public bathhouses with plumbing.

Christians scorned Islam, the Moors' religion, but the two religions had much in common. Both stressed personal morality, compassion, and charity. Muslims and Christians alike believed in heaven and hell.

The Moors usually did not force Christians to become Muslims. Christians had the choice of converting, paying a yearly tribute, or dying. Few Christians chose the third route. Spanish Jews, a well-educated, prosperous group, were mostly left in peace.

In most cases Muslims and Christians lived without much trouble. Nevertheless, Spanish Christians wanted to rule the country themselves. The Moors had set up governments at Cordova, Seville, and Granada. At first these governments answered to the Caliph (KAL-uhf) of Baghdad. He was a Muslim ruler who lived thousands of miles away in the Middle East. After a while Spain had its own Caliph in Cordova. Caliphs ruled Spain until 1031, when the system collapsed. Then the Moors split their territory into more than 20 different states.

Once divided, the Moors were easier to attack. Christians kept fighting until they had narrowed Muslim rule to one kingdom in the south—Granada.

Christians Unite. In 1469 Ferdinand of Aragon (AR-uh-gone) married Isabella of Castile (kass-TEEL). This marriage united members of two ruling families. Now much of northern Spain was ruled by one Christian family.

Ferdinand and Isabella were determined to make all of Spain Christian. This meant taking Granada from the Moors. The kingdom was about 200 miles long and 65 miles wide. It had 15 cities and 99 fortified towns. Beyond were rich green fields, olive trees, and vineyards. Mountains protected Granada on three sides. On the fourth side it faced the Mediterranean Sea.

In 1481, the Moors attacked a Christian fortress near Granada. Ferdinand and Isabella decided to strike back. First they assembled an army. They asked every noble and town in Christian Spain to send men. They searched other parts of Europe for more recruits. Reminded of earlier struggles against Muslims—the Crusades—many European nobles sent help.

The army's first target was the Moorish city of Malaga (MAL-uh-guh). It was a major port along the Mediterranean coast. Ships from Malaga had been able to slip past the Spanish. Then they would sail to North Africa. From there, these ships brought arms and food to keep Granada alive.

Ferdinand moved on Malaga in 1487 with 70,000 men. For three months his cannons fired away at the city's northern walls. Malaga was well supplied. It held out week after week. But finally the city surrendered. Its people became captives. Its treasures fell to the Spanish crown.

Granada Falls. By 1491, the days of the Moors seemed numbered. In Granada, the young king Boabdil (bo-ub-DEEL) must have known that time was running out. His city was full of refugees and the remains of the Moorish army. They wanted to keep up the fight. Boabdil led them in raids into Christian territory.

In the spring of 1491, the Spaniards camped outside Granada. They destroyed the surrounding farms to cut off the Moors' food supply. But Ferdinand would not attack. He and Isabella hoped to take Granada without loss of blood.

One night a fire started in the Spanish army camp. The fire spread and burned the entire camp. Ferdinand and Isabella decided to rebuild the camp in stone. They laid out the streets and buildings in the form of a cross. Then they painted all the stonework white so that the Moors would see the cross from a distance.

The Moors saw it, and it discouraged them. At first small groups of them tried to fight the Christians. But Boabdil finally

SPAIN BECOMES A NATION

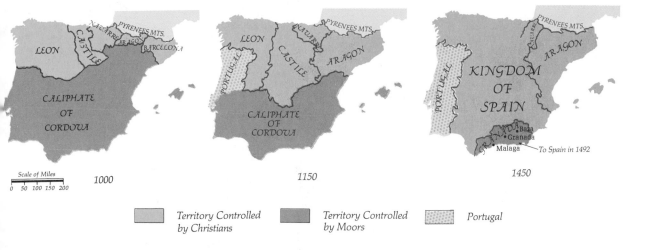

1000

1150

1450

Scale of Miles
0 50 100 150 200

Territory Controlled by Christians

Territory Controlled by Moors

Portugal

These three maps show the decline of Moorish power in Spain and the growth of Spain as a unified Christian nation. Use the map to answer the following questions.

1. In the year 1000, which group controlled most of Spain?

2. By the middle of the fifteenth century, which group ruled most of Spain?

3. In which year was Castile larger—1000 or 1150?

4. By 1150 what new nation appears on the western coast?

decided to seek an agreement with his enemies. On January 2, 1492, he rode out of Granada. Ferdinand and Isabella waited on the plain outside with their army. With tears in his eyes, Boabdil handed them the keys to his palace. The Christian monarchs waited while an advance guard rode into Granada. Soon, over the rooftops, atop a high tower, they saw a silver cross rise.

From Ferdinand and Isabella's time onward, Spain has remained a united Christian nation. Yet many of its old Christian kingdoms kept some of their independence. At times they even rebelled against the Spanish monarchy.

No Tolerance. The Moors did not fare well in Christian Spain. At first they were given a choice of leaving the country or becoming Christians. Later, even those who became Christians were treated poorly. In 1609 they were driven out of Spain.

In 1478, with the permission of the pope, Ferdinand and Isabella began the Inquisition (in-kwuh-ZISH-un). It was a campaign against beliefs which differed from Church law. The pope at first encouraged it as a way to defend Christianity from Jewish and Moorish influences. But it soon became a powerful political and economic crusade mainly against Jews.

When people were brought to trial under the Inquisition, their property was seized. Then, they were usually tortured and made to confess to crimes against Christianity. For example, Jews were ac-

cused of damaging Christian shrines. Even Jews who had converted to Christianity were not safe. They were acccused of practicing Judaism in secret. People were tortured until they accused other people.

Many Christians took advantage of the Inquisition. A Christian who was angry at a Jew could accuse him or her of profaning Christian beliefs. Priests and government officials grew wealthy off property taken from suspects.

In the same year that Granada was captured, all Jews who would not become Christians were expelled. In losing the Moors and the Jews, Spain lost some of its wealthiest and ablest people. It also lost many active members of its middle class. Thus, religious intolerance brought an end to a golden age of learning. Art, literature, science, and trade suffered. Christianity ruled supreme in Spain, but at a great cost.

✎ Quick Check

1. *Who were the Moors? When did they invade Spain? Why were they able to assume power?*

2. *Name three improvements the Moors brought to Spain. How did the Moors treat the Jews? The Christians? How did the Christians feel about the Moors?*

3. *In 1469, what event united northern Spain? What was the last Moorish kingdom in Spain? What happened to it? When?*

4. *What was the purpose of the Inquisition? How was it used against non-Christians? What was the cost to Spain?*

12
Russia's Two Ivans

Suddenly there was the sound of galloping horses. Then a crowd of horsemen thundered down upon the peaceful village. They slashed to left and right as they galloped, striking down men, women, and children. Then, as quickly as the invaders had come, they rode away. Every building had been burned to the ground.

That was what happened again and again in Russia in the Middle Ages. The villagers were Russians. The invaders were Tartars, a Mongol people from the plains of central Asia. Mongol warriors never attacked unless they were sure they could win. And they rarely left an enemy alive.

The Tartars came to Russia to expand their empire. In those days Russia was a slice of eastern Europe which stretched from the Baltic Sea to the Black Sea (see map p. 89). When the Mongols first arrived, Russia's leading city was Kiev (KEE-ehf). Under Mongol control a smaller city began to grow in importance. This city was Moscow, capital of the state of Muscovy.

Many Conquests. Moscow was governed by the Grand Princes of Muscovy. Ivan III was known as Ivan the Great. He became Grand Prince of Moscow in 1462. He added to the family land in every way possible—by war, purchase, treaty, or marriage. Under Ivan, Moscovy grew to be about three times the size of Texas.

In 1472, Ivan made a very clever marriage. He wed Zoe Paleologue (pah-LAY-uh-log), niece of the last Byzantine emperor. Byzantine rulers had absolute power over their subjects. After marrying Zoe, Ivan assumed the same kind of total power as the Byzantine rulers. Zoe encouraged him in this. She also insisted that he call himself "czar of all Russia."

St. Basil's Cathedral, built during Ivan IV's reign, still graces Moscow.

The word *czar* (zahr) was a Slavic form of the Latin *caesar*. It meant a ruler with supreme worldly and spiritual power.

The Tartars continued to trouble Moscow. But by 1480, Ivan felt strong enough to defy them. He refused to pay them their usual tribute. Russian and Tartar armies started to march toward each other. They met at the Ugra River. Neither side wanted to strike the first blow. In the end, both armies simply turned around and went home. Ivan claimed a victory, and the Tartars, for the time being, left Russia alone.

Besides expanding Russia, Ivan wanted to create political and religious order. He made laws which governed all of Russia. Although he refused an alliance with the pope, he was very pious. In Moscow, he built the Kremlin, an enclosed area holding six magnificent churches. The churches had onion-shaped roofs covered in gold leaf. They still stand today.

The Russian Church had grown out of the Orthodox Church of the Byzantine Empire. That empire collapsed when Constantinople fell to the Turks in 1453. The Russians believed that the leadership of the Church had been passed on to them. Later Russian rulers made their conquests in the name of Christianity.

A Feudal Land. Most importantly, though, Ivan set up a social order in Russia. It was to last for centuries. He granted land to nobles called *boyars*. In return, they had to give Ivan military service. The boyars mostly benefited from

Ivan IV increased Russia's territory and his own power.

the arrangement. The peasants who worked their lands did not. Before Ivan's rule, they rented land and were free to leave if they wished. Now they were serfs, legally bound to the land.

Ivan's grandson, Ivan IV, expanded Russia even further. He was determined to increase his own political authority. That meant destroying the power of the Russian nobles. Ivan had many members of the old nobility put to death. His use of terror earned him the title Ivan the Terrible.

To some Russians, though, Ivan IV was a hero. He ruled a vast territory to the east and southwest of Moscow. During his reign, contact was made with the West. The English opened a route to Moscow by way of the Arctic Ocean and the White Sea.

In 1584, Queen Elizabeth of England sent several representatives to Ivan IV. Suppose that one of them recorded his impressions in a letter to his wife:

May 19, 1584

My dearest Rosalind,

Today we met with Czar Ivan for the first time. He seems to be a rather old, tired man. But he was very glad to see us. He spoke of how he wants to trade with England. He is especially interested in buying weapons from us.

I'm lucky that I managed to learn some Russian on the ship coming here. The court gossip is very exciting. Everyone is nervous. They say that the czar is crazy. No one can predict what he'll do next.

Today I overheard some old servants talking about Ivan's life. They say he had a very unhappy childhood. After his father and mother died, the boyars took power. They mistreated Ivan till he was 14. Then, he had himself crowned czar. Ever since then, he has mistrusted the boyars.

Ivan was happy after he married for the first time. His wife was a noble-woman named Anastasia. They say he loved her very much. While they were married, Ivan was a very successful ruler. The serfs liked him because he cut their taxes. He let towns and villages choose their own officials. And he organized a good army. He conquered many lands and protected Moscow from the Tartars.

Everything changed when his wife died. The nobles say that she died naturally. But Ivan was convinced that she was poisoned. That was when he started to earn himself the title Ivan the Terrible. He dismissed his good advisors. He trusted no one. He married six different women and divorced them all.

At one point, he threatened to abandon the throne. When the people begged him to return, he began to act like a madman. He started to make fun of the Church. He hired 6,000 men and dressed them as monks. But instead of doing good deeds and praying, Ivan's "monks" did nothing but steal from and terrorize Russians. They killed and tortured many boyars and the clergy.

Tartars took advantage of this disorder to attack Russian cities and towns. They even burned down most of Moscow. At least the beautiful Kremlin was saved.

But the most terrible thing was yet to come. Two years ago, Ivan's first son and heir got his father angry. Ivan hit the boy over the head with a heavy stick. He was sorry afterwards, but his son died. Now everyone is worried about what will happen after Ivan dies. His other son, Fedor, appears to be simpleminded. They say he could never rule Russia.

I predict that there will be a great deal of unrest here very soon. Ivan looks like he will not live much longer. I only hope that we can make a trade agreement quickly.

Your loyal husband,

William

Alexander Nevski, a Russian saint and hero, with his family. As duke of Novgorod, he became famous for turning back the invading Swedes.

Ivan died the same year as the visit of Queen Elizabeth's representatives. Under his leadership, Russia doubled in size. But a great deal of blood was spilled.

As many people predicted, Fedor could not rule Russia. The crown went through many different hands in the years to follow. The Russian people would wait years for another strong ruler.

1. *Who were the Tartars? Why did they invade Russia? What city did they control?*

2. *What did Ivan III accomplish? Whom did he marry? How did she influence him? Where does the word* czar *come from?*

3. *What kind of social order did Ivan III set up? Who were the boyars?*

4. *What did Ivan IV do to increase his power? What reasons for this action does the letter give? Name two good things that Ivan did for Russia. Give two ways he lived up to his name, "Ivan the Terrible."*

THE EXPANSION OF THE RUSSIAN EMPIRE

This map shows the growth of Russia to 1584. Use the map to answer the following questions.

1. Name one town that was added to Russia by Ivan III.

2. What body of water does the Volga river flow into?

3. How far is it from Moscow to Constantinople?

4. What sea lies directly south of the Ukraine?

13
The Black Death

In 1347 an Italian trading ship sailed into the port city of Messina. It had come from the Black Sea port of Caffa, in the East. The merchants of Messina greeted the ship at the harbor. They were amazed to find that many of the sailors were dead or dying of a strange new disease. In what seemed no time at all, this disease began to attack the people of Messina.

The disease was the *bubonic plague,* then known only as the Black Death. Its symptoms were horrible. Victims suffered severe pain, ugly swellings, and fever. In the end, they always died. Sometimes victims went to bed healthy and died before they woke up.

What had started in Messina soon spread like wildfire. Trading ships and travelers brought the plague to town after town. Country people visiting a town brought the plague home with them. A ship with an entire crew dead of the plague ran aground in Norway. The disease then spread through Scandinavia. In three years, hardly a country in Europe was spared.

Europeans in the fourteenth century knew little about medicine. Doctors could neither cure the plague nor prevent it. They prescribed "medicines" that often did more harm than good. Their best advice on how to avoid the plague was, "When plague strikes your town, flee quickly, go far, and come back slowly." Often doctors took their own advice.

Panic and Death. In the end, no one was really safe. The town poor, who lived in crowded, filthy slums, were more likely to die. But even the wealthy died of plague. Kings, princesses, nobles, and bishops died. Monks, nuns, and other women were especially at risk. They spent more time indoors, often in dirty houses.

So many people caught the plague that often nobody was left to nurse the sick or bury the dead. Family ties came to mean nothing. Priests refused to give last rites to the dying. An Italian, Agnolo di Tura, wrote about the fear, confusion, and despair of the times:

> Father abandoned child, wife husband, one brother another, for this plague seems to strike through breath and sight. And so they died. And none could be found to bury the dead for money or friendship. . . . I buried with my own hands five of my own children in a single grave. . . . No bells. No tears. This is the end of the world.

Mysterious Causes. Because germs were unknown, doctors had no idea what caused the plague. Some claimed that an earthquake in India had released poisonous gases into the air. Others believed that a strange arrangement of planets in the sky was the cause.

To most people, however, the explanation was simple. The plague was caused by God's anger at human beings. Some people were greedy, lied, committed adultery, or were irreverent. It was believed that God struck back with the plague.

Christians went to church and begged the Virgin Mary, symbol of mercy, to end the plague. Stern clergy warned people to avoid sinning. Drinking, gambling, and cursing were frowned upon. In an

Religious processions, like this one in Rome, were intended to ward off the plague.

effort to stop God's anger, some people tried to pay for the sins of everyone. They dressed in coarse cloth and prayed constantly. Groups of them went through city streets weeping and beating themselves with whips. These people were called *penitents*.

Other people tried to protect themselves by wearing good-luck charms, or by chanting special words. *Abracadabra* was considered a magic word. People had it written on a triangle of paper and wore it around their necks.

Casting Blame. There was one more tragic side effect to the plague. When it first appeared, there were all sorts of rumors about its cause. Some Christians claimed that the Jews were responsible. They said that Jews were poisoning Christians' wells.

The Jews were a traditional target for Christians in medieval Europe. They were not allowed to own land or work as *artisans*, or craftspeople. To earn a living, they were merchants and moneylenders. Many Jews were some of the richest and best-educated people in Europe. However, their religious practices were considered strange. Christians blamed them for Christ's death.

Under torture, Jews were made to confess and accuse other Jews. In some towns, they did not even get a trial. Hundreds were gathered together and burned alive. The penitents especially encouraged the murder of Jews. In Germany and some surrounding countries, most of the local Jews were killed. The king of Poland and the pope protested, but in vain. At last, Christians noticed that Jews died of plague just like everyone else. Eventually the murders stopped.

No effort to end the plague worked. From 1347 to 1351, it was estimated that a third of all Europeans died. In cities, the numbers were even greater. Paris lost 50,000 people, half its population. In some areas as much as 90 percent of the population was wiped out.

Not until centuries later did anyone find out what caused the Black Death. It was caused by a germ. The germ came from a small black Asian rat, or the fleas

Citizens of Tournai, France, carrying the coffins of those who died of plague.

that lived on the rat. The bite of this rat or its fleas started the plague.

The rats came on ships from the East. Once in Europe, their numbers swelled alarmingly. This was possible because there was a shortage of the rat's natural enemy, the cat. Earlier in the century, cats had been declared agents of the devil. They were killed in great numbers. Fourteenth century cat-haters never knew their mistake. Much later, when the cause of the plague was known, an English poet wrote regretfully, "These villainous false cats,/ Were made for mice and rats."

Great Changes. Deaths from the plague caused labor shortages all over Europe. The feudal system began to fall apart. Under the feudal system, a serf farmed a piece of land and gave much of the produce to a lord. With many serfs dead, the survivors could demand pay for their work. After the plague died down, many of them ran away from their lords' estates and moved into towns. In Britain, the labor shortage was so serious that landowners began to raise sheep instead of growing crops. This took fewer workers.

The Church was also affected by the plague. After it was over, people asked, "What kind of God would do this to us?" Many of the faithful thought that God had been too harsh.

Priests and monks were criticized because many of them had abandoned the sick and dying. Some of them had grown rich by selling holy *relics*, or remains.

These were supposed to be objects touched by Jesus, the Virgin Mary, or various saints. The buyers of holy relics were supposed to be pardoned for their sins. When the plague was over, the sellers of relics became very unpopular. Geoffrey Chaucer, a popular medieval writer, wrote a story about a relics salesman who was only interested in money and did not really believe in his relics.

Many people thought that they could not escape the plague. So they decided to live as fully as possible. They began to ask, "Why should we celebrate the glory of a God who has brought on us death and unhappiness? Why should we not celebrate the glory of the human beings who survived?"

These ideas were shocking to most people. Yet they spelled the end of an age of great religious faith. European life would never be quite the same again.

✎ **Quick Check**

1. *What disease spread through Europe in the fourteenth century? What were its symptoms? Name three things Europeans believed caused it.*

2. *What was a* penitent? *In what other ways did people try to protect themselves from illness?*

3. *How did the plague contribute to religious intolerance?*

4. *What actually caused the plague? Why did it spread so easily?*

5. *What two great changes occurred in Europe as a result of the plague?*

PART 2
Review and Skills Exercises

	A		B		C		D	EF	G		H	
1000		1100		1200		1300		1400		1500	1600	1700

Putting Events in Order

In Part 2 you read of wars, disputes, and changes in government that shaped the nations of Europe. On the time line above, letters are placed on the approximate dates when certain important events took place. Below is a list of events that occurred during the period shown on the time line. The events are not in order. Decide which event belongs with each letter, A–H. Write the letters on a sheet of paper. By each letter list the correct event. Refer to the text for help.

- Battle of Hastings is fought.
- Spanish Inquisition begins.
- King John signs Magna Charta.
- Joan of Arc leads French troops.
- Last Moors are driven from Spain.
- Hundred Years' War begins.
- Ferdinand and Isabella take Granada from Muslim ruler; Jews are driven from Spain.
- Ivan the Great begins rule in Russia.

Interpreting a Reading

Read the paragraphs below and answer the questions that follow.

The Jewish Ghettos

Imagine this scene in Europe in the 1400's: Night is falling on a busy city. People are hurrying to get home before sunset. Many are crowding through narrow gates. Soon a man will shut the gates and lock them from the outside. The gates will not be unlocked until sunrise. The people who live inside the gates are Jews. Their homes are crowded together behind high walls. They are part of a large city. But they are

94

allowed to live in only one place in the city—in this walled-off section called a *ghetto*. A ghetto is a section of a city where people of a particular minority group live.

For centuries, Jews had chosen to live in separate sections of European cities and towns. They wanted to live near one another so they could practice their religious beliefs and keep their customs alive. Living close together, Jewish neighbors helped each other and kept their heritage and traditions alive.

But by the 1400's, the Jews had no choice about where they lived. Beginning in the late Middle Ages, Jewish ghettos became places where the Jews had to live.

Intolerance spread throughout fifteenth-century Europe. Jews were severely persecuted. They were blamed for the plague. Laws restricting their activities were passed. The Jews were forced to live in walled ghettos. Other laws kept them from owning farms and limited them to certain kinds of work. In many places, Jews were required to wear special hats or badges to identify themselves as Jews.

By the 1800's, new ideas of freedom began to spread throughout Europe. Jews worked hard to gain the rights of citizenship. Slowly they won *emancipation*, or freedom, from the restrictions of former laws. Among the freedoms Jews won was the chance to live outside the ghettos.

1. What is a ghetto?

2. How were the lives of Jews in Europe restricted in the late Middle Ages?

3. How might a minority benefit from living together in a section of a city?

4. When did European Jews begin to gain some freedoms? Why?

Building Vocabulary

Each sentence below contains a word or term that is used incorrectly. Read each sentence carefully and decide which term makes the sentence incorrect. Then write the numbers 1–8 on a sheet of paper. By each number write the incorrect word or term. Then write the word or term from the list below that makes the sentence correct.

1. The Moors of northern France were descendants of Vikings.

2. Magna Charta was spoken in England at the time of the Norman invasion and is the basis for the English language.

3. In 1205, a ransom, an order from the pope, prohibited people in England from marrying, being baptized, or being buried with a proper Church service.

4. *Czar* means the eldest son of a French king.

5. In thirteenth-century England, the framework for government was created with the establishment of the cathedral.

6. The Spanish Antidote was a campaign against people whose beliefs differed from Church law.

7. Boyars were Russian peasants.

8. During the time of the plague in Europe, people called Visigoths beat themselves in an effort to make up for the sins of everyone.

Modern	Normans	interdict
Parliament	serfs	Anglo-Saxon
Inquisition	dauphin	penitents

PART
3

THE
RENAISSANCE

In 1425 a teacher named Vittorino da Feltre (veet-oh-REE-no dah FAIL-trah) set up a school for boys in the Italian city of Mantua (MAN-chuh-wuh). His goal, he said, was to turn out "the complete man." Such a man would not only know how to read and write. He would also have a good character, a healthy body, and an able mind.

To form good character, Vittorino gave the boys religious training. To create healthy bodies, he drilled his students in gymnastics. To develop their minds, Vittorino taught them mathematics, Greek, and Latin.

Not all of Vittorino's ideas were new ones. But his school was very different from most medieval schools. Earlier schools had trained men to be priests and clerks to serve the Church. Vittorino trained his students to live well in the world. He wanted them to be able to make the right choices and act on those choices. His ideas soon became popular.

These ideas were part of a whole new spirit which had come to Italy by 1425. People wanted to learn more about human beings and the world in which they lived. They were eager to develop their talents. They also wanted to study nature. All this led them to try to improve their earthly lives. Because of this new emphasis on human activity, scholars of the time were called *humanists*. They

Vittorino da Feltre (above) taught the new humanism. "Portrait of a Youth" by Filippino Lippi (right). Page 96: Detail from Gozzoli's "Procession of the Magi" uses a Medici for his biblical king.

shared many values with the thinkers of ancient Greece and Rome. So they took an intense interest in the art and writings of that time.

This new spirit lasted from about 1300 to 1600. Historians have named this period the *Renaissance* (ren-uh-SAHNS). The term comes from a French word meaning "rebirth." During the Renaissance there was a rebirth of learning. People believed that through learning they could achieve a happy life.

The people of the Renaissance did not turn away from Christianity. Most of

In the 16th century, students eagerly pursued astronomy and many other subjects.

them were still interested in leading Christian lives. They were still concerned about going to heaven after they died. But they also believed that while they were on earth they could live more reasonably and humanely.

Italy Leads. Although humanist ideas spread throughout Europe, they had their roots in Italy. Why there? The Crusades had encouraged trade. And trade between Europe and the East went through Italy. The Italian peninsula was closer to the Eastern lands. Italians were good sailors and expert shipbuilders. As a result, foreign products first came to Italy, and so did foreign ideas.

This trade led to the growth of Italian cities. Italians who lived in cities became more worldly. Traders and merchants grew wealthy. These people had more leisure time and more of a desire for life's comforts. They could afford the best in the arts.

Italian travelers were the first to find old books in out-of-the-way places. Italian humanists studied and translated Greek and Roman works. Because books were so expensive, few people could enjoy them. However, in the fifteenth century the printing press was developed. This made books available in greater numbers and at lower cost. Thus, Renaissance ideas reached all corners of Europe.

During the Renaissance, people welcomed new ideas. There was a burst of activity, including new inventions and bold explorations. Plays, stories, and poems were written in everyday language, and painting and sculpture were done in a new style. Medieval painters and sculptors had worked mostly in churches. They had tried to express religious ideas and feelings. Now artists also turned to the world around them.

Renaissance artists wanted to show the world as it really was. They saw that men and women were not all beautiful and not all good. They painted people as they saw them—sometimes ugly, sometimes not. They wanted people to look into a picture as if it were a window. So they discovered ways to give pictures depth. They learned how to show movement in an entirely natural-looking way. And they applied their new techniques to many subjects, including religious ones.

The Renaissance was a time of hope for all kinds of undertakings. It was also a time for many searching questions about human behavior. The spirit of the age was expressed by one of its most famous poets, Francesco Petrarch (fran-CHESS-koe PEH-trark). "For what . . . will it profit to have known the nature of beasts, . . . but to be ignorant of . . . the nature of man — why we are born, where we come from, and where we go."

14
The Medici: Rulers of Florence

In medieval Europe, a person's life was largely determined by birth. Serf children became poor serfs. Noble children usually became wealthy and powerful. However, with the breakdown of the feudal system, this was no longer always true. A lucky peasant family could work its way to great wealth. Anyone with a little money might become rich by cleverly buying and selling. This was especially true in towns such as Florence in Italy.

Florence was a true Renaissance city. It became a center of commerce, learning, and art. The city's wealth was based on its cloth trade. Some Florentine merchants bought undyed woolen cloth from the Netherlands. Then they dyed it in brilliant colors. Other merchants wove and dyed silk. Still others sewed ready-made clothing, which was a new item. Most clothes were still made at home.

Market Rules. Merchants protected their success by setting up trade *guilds*. These organizations set the prices of goods and the wages for those who made them. Guilds were also responsible for setting standards of quality. They restricted the activities of foreign merchants and artisans. For example, you could not make boots in Florence unless you belonged to the right guild. Then you could only sell them if they met the standard of quality.

Only one fifth of Florentines were allowed to belong to guilds. The other four fifths were mostly poor workers and servants. Although these people worked hard for little money, rich guild members thought that they should not complain. One wrote, "If the lowest order of society earn enough food to keep them going from day to day, then they have enough."

The money changer (bottom) belonged to a guild, unlike these market workers (top) and most common Florentines.

Making money was extremely important to Florentines. "He who has no possessions is regarded as an animal" was a popular saying in Florence. The rich looked down on anyone who had not been lucky enough to make or inherit money.

With the growth of trade in Florence, a family named Medici (MED-uh-chee) became very powerful. Originally a peasant family, the Medici began to grow wealthy in the twelfth century. They made their money by buying and selling cloth and other goods. They also set up banks in Florence and other cities. By the fifteenth century, they were the leading family in Florence. They greatly influenced city life and politics. Although they feuded constantly with other wealthy families, they usually came out on top. All in all, they were clever and ruthless people.

The basis of the Medici power was gold. Family bankers lent money not only to businessmen, but also to kings they favored. The Church did not allow lenders to charge interest on loans. But they could charge for "late repayments." In the end, this amounted to the same thing as interest.

Love of Life. The Medici gave a great deal of money to the Church and the poor. They were known for throwing lavish festivals. Everyone, rich or poor, was invited. Many Medici were also talented men and women who appreciated the talents of others. They supported poor young artists and collected the finest pieces for their palaces. Some of the most famous works of art of the Renaissance were paid for by Medici money.

In addition, the Medici loved learning. One family leader, Cosimo, would do almost anything to get a new book. Before the printing press was developed books were scarce. Each book had to be copied

103

Lorenzo de Medici, ruler of Florence and patron of the arts.

icent. High-spirited, energetic, and talented, Lorenzo was the ideal of a well-educated, cultured, Renaissance gentleman.

Despite his wealth and many talents, Lorenzo was very modest. For a Medici, he lived simply. At parties, he chose guests for their talents rather than for their wealth or rank. He always addressed the poor and lowborn as his equals. At one party, Lorenzo completely forgot his guests when he wandered away to talk with a peasant farmer.

Lorenzo was popular, but he had some powerful enemies. One was a friar named Savonarola (sav-uh-nuh-ROH-luh), who preached against the Medici family. He hated them because they encouraged people to pursue money and earthly pleasures. Savonarola considered this immoral. The friar attacked Lorenzo as a corrupter of young people. He even said that the study of the classics encouraged a return to pre-Christian beliefs. Some Florentines listened to Savonarola and publicly burned playing cards, make-up, and paintings of nude people.

The rival Pazzi (PAHT-zee) family also hated the Medici. When Lorenzo was a young man, the Pazzi plotted to kill him. The Pazzi thought that the Medici had ruled Florence long enough. Pope Sixtus IV himself supported the plot against the Medici. The Pazzi persuaded two corrupt priests to stab Lorenzo and his brother Giuliano (joo-lee-YAH-no) while they prayed in the cathedral. Lorenzo escaped with a wound, but Giuliano was killed.

and illustrated by hand. Cosimo traveled all over Europe to buy them. Once he paid off a bankrupt friend's debts. He asked in return only that the friend will him his private library. When he had gathered about 800 books, Cosimo opened the first public library in Europe. His fellow scholars especially prized the *classics*, or books by ancient Greek and Roman writers.

Cosimo's grandson, Lorenzo, took after his grandfather in his love of art and learning. He lived from 1449 to 1492. Historians now call him Lorenzo the Magnif-

The people were furious at the men who had dared to attack their beloved Lorenzo. They tortured and killed all Pazzi who had been involved in the plot. The Pazzi family was disgraced, and Lorenzo became more popular than ever.

Like his grandfather Cosimo, Lorenzo supported artists. He paid them well for their work, and considered the money well spent.

A portrait of Giuliano de Medici, by Botticelli.

New Focus in Art. While the Medici ruled Florence, Florentine artists were developing a new style of art. Formerly, medieval art had dealt mostly with religious subjects. Artists painted and sculpted religious scenes in a flat, one-dimensional style. The result was often beautiful but unrealistic.

In the fourteenth century, a painter named Giotto di Bondone (JAH-toh dee bahn-DOHN-ay) began to paint in a new way. Giotto painted saints and sinners as real people. He especially tried to make them show human emotions. Giotto was able to do this by using light and dark shadings. He painted shadows to make objects look real.

After Giotto died, some artists took further steps away from the medieval style. They began to show the human body in their work.

Botticelli, (baht-ih-CHEL-lee) in his *Birth of Venus*, painted a scene from Roman mythology. Lorenzo de Medici praised the painting and bought it. But he had his eye on another artist. In 1483, he set up a school for promising young artists. One of the pupils was the 13-year-old Michelangelo (my-kuh-LAN-juh-loh). Lorenzo became so sure of Michelangelo's talent that he raised him as his own son. Michelangelo became famous for his statues and for painting the ceiling of the Sistine Chapel in Rome. His work shows that he carefully studied *anatomy*, or the make-up of the body. Then he improved upon it to produce the perfect human being.

The rule of Lorenzo the Magnificent was a high point for the Medici. After he died, the country was torn by a long war with France. Lorenzo's son Piero had no talent to rule. The writer Machiavelli (see Chapter 16) said that Lorenzo's death was doubly sad, since only he could have brought peace back to Italy.

Some of Lorenzo's descendants became very famous. One of his sons became Pope Leo X. A great-granddaughter became queen of France. Then fortunes changed, and the family's power declined. The last of the Medici died in 1743, having left to the city of Florence one of the world's great art collections.

*Giotto's "The Lamentation of Christ"
(left). Michelangelo's David (above),
stands proud and a bit scornful, a new
model for the people of the Renaissance,
as is Botticelli's beautiful Flora (right).*

✎ Quick Check

1. Why did Renaissance people have more of a chance to improve their lives than medieval people?

2. What European city was a true Renaissance city? What made it so?

3. What were guilds? Name some of the market rules set up by the guilds.

4. What family had great influence in Florence in the fifteenth century? How did they earn their wealth? On what kinds of things did they spend it?

5. What did Giotto di Bondone try to show in his paintings? After Giotto, what further steps did artists take away from medieval art?

6. Who did Lorenzo Medici raise as his own son?

15
A Man of Many Talents

He could draw an angel, the insides of a clock, or the design for a bridge. The angel would be beautiful, the clock would work, and the bridge would hold up in the wind.

Who was this remarkable person? He was Leonardo da Vinci (lee-oh-NAR-doe dah VIN-chee). Leonardo was the ideal Renaissance man. He tried almost everything and brought a stroke of genius to each of his projects.

Leonardo lived from 1452 to 1519. He was a painter, sculptor, engineer, architect, musician, and mechanic all in one. He had so many ideas that he could not work on all of them at once. He wrote them down in his notebooks. Then he went on to other things.

As a boy, Leonardo was curious about everything. He collected enough animals, plants, flowers, leaves, and bones to fill his father's house. Then he drew them all, over and over.

When Leonardo was 15, his family recognized his talent. They brought him to the celebrated painter Verrocchio (vehr-ROW-kyo), who ran a workshop in Florence. Verrocchio accepted him as his *apprentice*, or assistant.

Florence was a great center of Renaissance art, partly because of the Medici family. It was filled with busy workshops where artisans worked their trades. Back then, an artist was really a master craftsperson—skillful with tools and materials. In the spirit of their time, artists seemed always to be trying out new designs and processes.

Student Becomes a Master. Leonardo surprised his master with his skillful drawings and beautiful paintings. In fact, Verrocchio decided that Leonardo was a better painter than he was. So he gave up painting for goldsmithing. By the time Leonardo was 28, he was considered one of the finest painters of his time.

In later years, he painted the *Mona Lisa* and the *Virgin of the Rocks*. Lovers of Renaissance art often regret that Leonardo did not paint more. Also, he often did not finish what he had begun. He would get bored or become interested in doing something else. Less than a dozen of Leonardo's paintings survive.

Leonardo was especially good at painting people because he studied anatomy. He probably knew more about how the human body looked and worked than any other person at that time. He used his knowledge about what was going on inside the body to make the outside look more real. He was also able to show motion because he understood how muscles worked.

To gain such a detailed understanding of the body, Leonardo dissected corpses. The drawings he made from his studies were so accurate that some of them are still used in medical textbooks.

One of Leonardo's remarkable qualities was that he could apply his knowledge to many different areas. For example, he loved to play music and design musical instruments. His flutes were modeled after the human larynx, or voice box, which he had discovered while studying anatomy.

Francesco Melzi (fran-CHESS-koe MELT-zee) was one of Leonardo's favorite students. In 1499, he might have written a letter like this to his mother:

Verona, 1499

Dear Mother,

I hope you haven't worried too much about our getting hurt in the capture of Milan (meh-LAN). The soldiers left our workshop alone as soon as the captain heard it was Leonardo's. He even asked Leonardo to do a painting for him. But Leonardo guessed that the fighting would soon resume. So, one dark night, we slipped out of town.

Since then, I've heard that the soldiers ruined Leonardo's beautiful statue of a horse. It stood in the open square of the city. It was huge—about three stories high. The soldiers used it for target practice! Leonardo is very sad because the statue was really a mold. He has wanted to cast the horse in bronze for many years.

I am worried about the safety of The Last Supper. *Leonardo has just finished painting it on the wall of a monastery dining room. Nothing on earth is so lifelike! You can almost step into the picture. Each of the 12 apostles shows his personality in his face or by the way he stands or sits.*

We have had no trouble finding work since we left Milan. Everywhere we stop, people ask Leonardo to paint something for them. But instead, he is wasting his time again. I can tell you about it, but don't breathe a word to anyone else. People will think we are crazy.

Leonardo has built a set of **wings**. Yes, wings. I knew that he had been watching birds, but never dreamed that this would come of it. He has set up a device made of pulleys on boards. When I get in it and move my arms and legs, I make the wings fan out. Now we go together very quietly into the country. At the top of a hill, I get into his wings and try to fly. It hasn't worked yet. I keep hoping it will.

All my friends think I am learning to be an artist. What would they say if they saw how we really spend our time? I hope Leonardo gets back to work soon. If he does, we may get a chance to go to Rome. All the best artists are there, working for the pope.

Here are some gold coins Leonardo gave me. Love to the family.

Your son,
Francesco

The only known likeness of Leonardo is this self-portrait (left). His masterpiece, "The Last Supper" (above). In his notebooks, he described in detail his idea for a wing mechanism (below).

Francesco Melzi remained loyal till his teacher died. Leonardo left him his notes in his will. Francesco could not develop Leonardo's ideas, but he knew that the notebooks were valuable. He preserved them with great care. He organized some

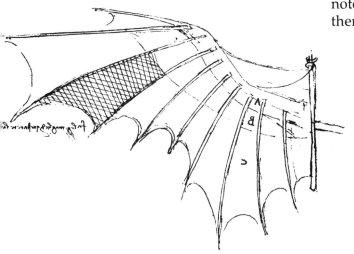

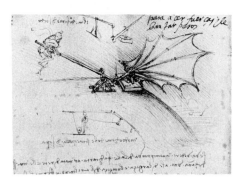

111

of the notes into a book about painting methods, which was published a century later.

Unfortunately, Francesco's sons realized the value of the notebooks. Gradually, they sold them. Some were lost.

Leonardo's Foresight. What made Leonardo's notebooks valuable? They show the thoughts and ideas of the man many scholars recognize as the first modern scientist. In his time most thinkers still tried to find things out by reading the Bible and classical literature. Leonardo preferred to discover things by observing and experimenting. For him, even painting was a kind of science.

"He was like a man who awoke too early in the darkness, while all others were still asleep." So wrote Sigmund Freud (froyd) centuries later in his famous psychological study of Leonardo. Indeed, Leonardo's observations and inventions were often too advanced. As an engineer, he drew many useful things. But many designs remained hidden in his notebooks until recently. Other inventors who lived centuries later built similar things, not knowing that Leonardo had designed them first.

For example, he drew the first bicycle. The design was very much like bicycles today. Three centuries later, people began to build bicycles. The earliest ones had one big wheel and one small wheel. Naturally, they were very hard to ride. It took many years before inventors arrived at the modern design that Leonardo had already perfected.

Some of Leonardo's designs did get used in his time and after. He designed the gig mill, a machine used in making woolen cloth. It did a lot of work with little effort. During the Industrial Revolution centuries later, workers rioted against its use. They feared the gig mill would put them out of work.

Leonardo's remaining notebooks are scattered about Europe in various libraries. They are difficult to read because Leonardo wrote many things in "mirror" writing. This is writing that can only be read by looking at it in a mirror.

In his notes, Leonardo once summed up the aim and purpose of his work. He wrote, "O investigator, do not flatter yourself that you know the workings of nature, but rejoice in knowing the purpose of those things designed by your own mind."

✎ **Quick Check**

1. *When did Leonardo da Vinci live? Why is he considered an ideal Renaissance man? List his skills.*

2. *Name three of Leonardo da Vinci's paintings. Describe three inventions from his notebooks that were used centuries later.*

3. *Why was Leonardo so good at painting people accurately?*

4. *Who was Francesco Melzi? What did Leonardo leave to him in his will, and why were they important? What happened to these items?*

5. *Where did Renaissance people usually turn to answer their questions? What did Leonardo use instead?*

16
The Master of Politics

Niccolo Machiavelli (NICK-oh-low mack-yuh-VELL-ee) spent many weary days wishing he were somewhere else. He rose early, as everyone did in the small Italian town of San Casciano (sahn kah-SHAH-noh) in 1513. All day he looked after his land. It was barely large enough to support his family of six children. From time to time, he gazed over the fields to the rooftops of Florence. That was where he wanted to be, but he was not allowed to go there.

Machiavelli had been one of Florence's leading patriots. In his writings, he had defended its *republican* form of government. This meant that the ruler, Piero Soderini, was elected by the people. Machiavelli had worked as Soderini's secretary for 14 years. Mainly, Machiavelli had organized the military. He believed that it was important to have a strong army on hand at all times.

In 1512, the army Machiavelli had organized lost a battle. The Florentine soldiers were supposed to defend the town of Prato against invading Spanish. But the Spanish army was too strong. They looted and burned the city, killing thousands in their path. Soderini, humiliated at his army's failure, resigned in disgrace.

Thrown Out. A new ruler rode into Florence. He was Giuliano de Medici, son of Lorenzo the Magnificent. The Medici family had lost much of their influence and no longer controlled Florence. Giuliano intended to change that. First, he got rid of Soderini's old supporters. He threw Machiavelli into jail, where he was tortured.

113

Machiavelli was soon freed, but his political career seemed over. He had been too close to the old rulers to be trusted by the new ones. Although he wanted to keep working in government, the Medici did not trust him. But he loved the game of power so much that he kept thinking about it.

In the evenings, he read about Greek and Roman rulers of old. He compared them with the rulers of his time. He wrote down the advice he would give to these rulers, if he were in a position to do so. The following ideas are taken from *The Prince*, Machiavelli's most famous book.

A man who wants to be a ruler had better enlist and train his own soldiers. He must depend on himself and his own resources alone. The Italian duke Cesare Borgia [say-ZAR BOR-jiuh], who died a few years ago, learned this. He is a good example for other rulers to follow.

At the end of the last century, Pope Alexander VI wished to set up his relative, Cesare Borgia, with a kingdom of his own. But how to get it? None of the other rulers in Italy wished to see the pope or his family grow more powerful. So the pope made friends with the king of France, who lent Cesare some soldiers. With these, Cesare won the Romagna [roh-MAHN-yah], an area in northeastern Italy.

Cesare knew that he must become independent of both the king and the pope. So he brought the captains of his army to his side by giving them money and land. He killed those in Romagna whose property he had taken. Their followers were frightened into joining the Borgia side.

Cesare named Remirro de Orco [reh-MEER-oh duh OR-coe], a cruel but efficient man, governor of Romagna. He quickly brought the people of Romagna to heel. After the land was peaceful, Cesare wanted to get rid of Remirro, who was a potential rival. Then he would look like a hero to the people of Romagna.

One morning, the people found Remirro's body in the middle of the public square. It had been cut in two. A bloody knife lay beside it. Then Cesare replaced Remirro with an easier governor. Yet he kept the power in his own hands.

Cesare Borgia had planned well to secure Romagna. He then turned to conquering the other Italian states, one by one. But at a crucial point in his plan, he fell ill. He could not defend himself, so he lost all.

It was bad luck that defeated him, not bad planning. His actions show what a new ruler must do to keep his conquests. First, a newcomer must kill the entire family of the previous ruler. If he does not, they will always be plotting against him. And second, he must not raise taxes or change laws.

In this way most people will find that their daily lives have changed very little. There will always be grumblers, but they cannot do much without the help of others. And most people will not stir themselves if they have not been harmed. The few who are killed are soon forgotten. In fact, a man remembers the loss of his father's property longer than his father's death.

A ruler may wish to be good. But the world is full of people who are not good. So a ruler should be ready to do evil if he must. If he dreams of a world in which good always wins, he will be ruined.

Machiavelli (above) dedicated his book The Prince *to Lorenzo de Medici.*

It is enough to *appear* to be good. Let circumstances decide whether goodness is the right course. If people will not follow laws, they must be forced. So let us learn from the fox and the lion. The lion roars to frighten off wolves, but he has no defense against a trap. The fox is wary of traps, but wolves can beat him. The ruler who wants to survive must be a lion at some times, a fox at others. He must frighten people some times, trick them at others. This is the way things are.

At about the same time Machiavelli wrote *The Prince*, he wrote another set of essays. In them, he again praised the republican form of government and criticized "the enemies of virtue." Yet there was no hint of this thinking in *The Prince*.

Machiavelli died in 1572. In his last years, he was allowed to take some part in government work. Florentine leaders sent him on some missions, and he continued to write. But his most famous work remained *The Prince*. It was shocking when first published, and still is. It very quickly gave Machiavelli a bad name. To be "Machiavellian" means to be cleverly dishonest. Yet Machiavelli himself seems to have been a decent person. His advice came from what he himself saw and experienced.

Machiavelli's work was the beginning of modern *political science*, or the study of government. After him, Europeans began to look more closely at what really happens in government. They began to think about ways to make government more moral.

✎ Quick Check

1. *What happened to Machiavelli after Giuliano de Medici became the ruler of Florence?*

2. *In* The Prince, *what defeated Cesare Borgia? According to Machiavelli, what must a newcomer do to keep his conquests?*

3. *What does it mean to be "Machiavellian"? Find a sentence in* The Prince *to support your answer.*

4. *After Machiavelli, how did Europeans begin to think about government?*

17
All the World's A Stage

Every weekday morning in Stratford-on-Avon, England, the school bell rang at seven. Boys who had been waiting in the village square ran into school. They opened their books for eight long hours of studying Latin. If a student was very good, he might be allowed to study Greek.

This is the way boys were educated in much of Europe in the sixteenth century. Many great universities, including Oxford and Cambridge, were well established. But few students went beyond their village school.

Born in 1564, William Shakespeare went to the Stratford school and quit in his early teens to go to work. His family was poor and needed the money. Very little is known about his childhood. But he probably enjoyed bowling, archery,

and roaming the woods. No doubt he saw many plays, too.

When Shakespeare was 18, he married Anne Hathaway. They had several children together. Although he loved his family, Shakespeare was restless in Stratford. While his children were still babies, he went to live in London, 100 miles away.

An Actor's Life. London had a population of about 160,000. But it must have seemed huge to Shakespeare after tiny Stratford. Its narrow streets were crowded, dirty, and noisy. The ground floors of many houses were shops where merchants made and sold their wares. Peddlers came and went, calling out their goods. You could even buy sheet music from a peddler. Thieves passed through the crowds, picking pockets and purses.

117

To earn a living, Shakespeare joined an acting company called The Chamberlain's Men. The name fit because only men were allowed to appear on stage. Women's parts were played by teenage boys whose voices had not yet changed. Women were only allowed to attend plays.

Almost everybody could afford to go to the theater then. Standing room tickets cost a penny. Seats cost more, so most playgoers stood. Often they were rowdy,

Swan theater in London (left) where Shakespeare's plays were performed. Below, a band of players act out a farce.

because they knew a good play from a bad one. If a play did not please them, they might throw rotten fruit at the actors.

In the Middle Ages, most plays had been about morality and religion. They were intended to give guidelines on how to be a good Christian. English writers began to write a different kind of play around 1540.

In 1558, Queen Elizabeth I took the throne. She liked plays with humor, action, romance, and violence. She encouraged writers to write this way. Under her influence, productions became very expensive. Actors wore silk and velvet costumes. There were many changes of scenery.

Shakespeare found that being an actor was very hard. He had to learn his roles fast and remember many different parts. Sometimes he had to sell tickets and produce stage effects, like sound, wind, and rain. There were rewards for all his hard work, though. A good actor could become rich and famous.

Most theater companies had many problems. There were people in London who wanted to make acting illegal. An organization called The Common Council in London tried to shut down the theaters. They claimed that theaters caused "great disorders and inconveniences . . . unchaste, ugly, and shameless speeches and doings . . . a waste of money of the poor . . . and many other corruptions of youth." At one time, the theaters did shut down, but not for moral reasons. When the plague struck London in 1592, people were forbidden to meet in public. After the plague died down, the theaters reopened.

Another problem facing theater companies came from their success. The English often went to the theater. Any theater could count on a sellout just by advertising a new play. But Shakespeare's company never had enough new plays to perform. There were simply not enough writers to meet the demand.

Some well-educated playwrights created beautifully written plays. But these often lacked excitement. Other authors were uneducated, but their badly written plays had the excitement that audiences demanded. There was a need for a writer who had the "common touch" but could also write well.

Playwright for All. Shakespeare filled this need. He lacked a fine education, but he was a poet by nature. His career as an actor made him aware of what the audience wanted. One of his first plays, *A Comedy of Errors*, was just what Elizabethan audiences loved. Like many plays of the time, it was written mostly in verse. Its success encouraged Shakespeare to write more.

In a typical Shakespearean *comedy*, characters deal with various problems in a funny way. There are love triangles and people fooling each other with disguises. For example, in *Twelfth Night*, the heroine Viola is disguised as a boy for protection. She goes to work for Duke Orsino and falls in love with him. Unfortunately for

This engraving of William Shakespeare appeared in the front of the first printed volume of his plays published in 1623.

her, he is in love with a lady named Olivia, who ignores him. He sends Viola to bring messages of love to Olivia. Believing that Viola is a boy, Olivia falls in love with *her*. After all the confusion is sorted out, the play ends happily with a triple wedding.

Queen Elizabeth became a great admirer of Shakespeare. She often went to see his plays. After seeing *Henry IV* and laughing at the character of Falstaff, the queen commanded, "Write me another play with that drunken knight." Shakespeare agreed. Two years later he came out with *The Merry Wives of Windsor*, which featured an even funnier Falstaff.

In 1594, Shakespeare tried his hand at writing *tragedies*. In a tragedy, a hero or heroine struggles with a stronger force such as Time or Fate. Eventually, the force wins. The character is always strong and noble, but also has a weakness that speeds his or her downfall.

In 1601, Shakespeare wrote *Hamlet*, which most critics believe is his greatest tragedy. In it, Hamlet, the hero, meets the ghost of his father. The ghost tells him that he has been murdered by his own brother, Hamlet's uncle. Hamlet has to conceal his knowledge of the murder to protect his own life. He knows that he must murder his uncle in revenge, but is unable to do it. Why? He cannot make up his mind to do anything, which is his weakness. His indecision soon drives him insane. Or, he may be only pretending insanity. Throughout the play, the audience is never sure.

Soon after *Hamlet* was first performed, Queen Elizabeth died. Her cousin, King James I of Scotland, took the throne. At first it looked as if Shakespeare's career might be over. James was very conservative. In addition, he had the power to outlaw all acting companies from London. Surprisingly, James turned out to be an even more enthusiastic fan than Elizabeth. When Shakespeare's company presented *Macbeth*, which is set in Scotland, they won the Scottish king's heart.

Shakespeare pleased his king even more by writing new plays. Toward the end of his life, he began to experiment with a new kind of play. These were the *romances*, which were neither comic nor tragic. In them, Shakespeare tried to show a wide range of human emotions and experiences. *The Winter's Tale*, for example, mixes both comedy and tragedy. Like all the romances, it has a happy ending with a catch in it. A husband and wife are reunited after a long quarrel. But the audience cannot be sure whether the wife truly forgives the husband.

Shakespeare died in 1616 at the age of 52. No one is sure how many plays he wrote. Thirty-seven survive. In addition, he wrote two long poems and over 100 *sonnets*. These were 14-line poems with fixed rhyme patterns. Although his plays were not published in his lifetime, he always knew that his work would survive. He wrote, "Not marble, nor the gilded monuments/ Of princes, shall outlive this powerful rhyme." His plays are still performed all over the world.

✎ Quick Check

1. *What was Shakespeare's first job? Describe the theater in London at that time.*

2. *When did Queen Elizabeth I take the throne? What kinds of plays were popular before her time? What kind of changes occurred in the theater due to her influence?*

3. *Give two reasons why Shakespeare was a successful playwright in his time.*

4. *What do characters deal with in a typical Shakespearean comedy? A tragedy? A romance? Name one of Shakespeare's plays in each category.*

5. *How many of Shakespeare's plays survive? What else did he write besides plays?*

PART 3
Review and Skills Exercises

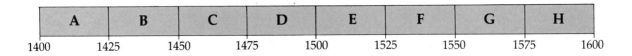

A	B	C	D	E	F	G	H

1400   1425   1450   1475   1500   1525   1550   1575   1600

Putting Events in Order

Part 3 described some of the people and ideas that were important in Europe beginning in the fourteenth century. There was a renewed interest in ancient civilizations. Scholars and thinkers studied such human activities as the arts, sciences, and government. The time line above has been divided into periods lettered A–H. On a sheet of paper write the numbers 1–6. Read the following list of events. Decide when each event occurred. By each number write the letter of the period when the event took place. You will not use all of the letters. Refer to your text to help you.

1. Machiavelli is jailed by Giuliano de Medici.

2. Lorenzo de Medici is born.

3. Lorenzo de Medici sets up a school for young artists; Michelangelo is a pupil.

4. Queen Elizabeth I begins her reign.

5. Leonardo da Vinci is accepted as an apprentice by Verrocchio.

6. The plague shuts London theaters.

Matching People with Deeds and Ideas

Write the numbers 1–10 on a sheet of paper. Beside each number, write the name from the list below that fits the description.

1. My Italian school for boys aimed at developing strong minds and bodies so that young men leaving the school would be able to live well.

2. As a famous poet, I expressed the spirit of the Renaissance in my work.

3. I was a ruler of Florence, and a cultured man who encouraged artists.

4. I was no friend of the Medicis. In fact, I preached against them and their encouraging of immoral ways.

5. You can thank me for bringing a change to art during the early Renaissance. I painted subjects in a way that made them look real.

6. *The Birth of Venus* is my painting. I worked to express the beauty of the human body in my paintings.

7. I painted the ceiling of the Sistine Chapel in the Vatican in Rome. I also created beautiful statues.

8. You can call me the true "Renaissance man," for I tried my hand at many things. I was a painter, sculptor, engineer, architect, musician, and mechanic.

9. My book, *The Prince,* shocked people because it states that a ruler may need to use harsh means to stay in power.

10. I was an actor, a poet, and a playwright, and my works pleased two English monarchs.

Botticelli	Savonarola
Machiavelli	Michelangelo
Lorenzo de Medici	Francesco Petrarch
Leonardo da Vinci	Shakespeare
Vittorino da Feltre	Giotto di Bondone

Building Vocabulary

Each sentence below contains two words or terms in parentheses. Write the numbers 1–10 on a sheet of paper. By each number write the word or term that best completes the sentence.

1. A revival of interest in learning and the flowering of the arts identify a period in history known as the (Middle Ages/Renaissance).

2. A(n) (humanist/inventor) is a scholar who is concerned with the values and interests of humans.

3. In Florence, merchants established organizations called trade (guilds/fairs) to control the production of goods.

4. The Medici family earned a reputation for giving (lavish/pagan) celebrations.

5. Renaissance painters were interested in the structure, or (anatomy/philosophy), of the human form.

6. The (cotton gin/gig mill) was an invention of Leonardo da Vinci's that helped in the making of cloth.

7. Even today we refer to someone who is cleverly dishonest as being (medieval/Machiavellian).

8. In a (republic/dictatorship), the leaders are chosen by the people.

9. If you were to study the way governments work, you would be studying (theology/political science).

10. A Shakespearian play that involves an unhappy ending for a hero or heroine is known as a (love triangle/tragedy).

PART
4

THE
REFORMATION

At the opening of the sixteenth century, nearly all western Europeans were united in their religion. They looked to the Roman Catholic Church for their beliefs. The Church was called Roman because it had its center in Rome. It was called Catholic, meaning universal, because all Christians of western Europe belonged to it. The Church was richer and in many ways more powerful than any single European king.

Europeans were still very religious in the year 1500. Salvation — or a happy life in heaven after death—was their final goal. To obtain it, they believed they had to take part in the sacraments (sacred acts) of the Church. Participating in the sacraments also gave Christians a feeling of religious unity.

The sacraments included baptism at birth, weekly confession, and the taking of communion. Unless a Christian belonged to the Church, he or she could not receive the sacraments. And without the sacraments, there could be no salvation. For example, during the communion ceremony a priest symbolically transformed bread and wine into the body and blood of Jesus Christ. This was called *transubstantiation*. People believed that after they ate the bread and drank wine, Christ forgave their sins. This helped pave the way to heaven.

Only a priest could give communion, hear confessions, or baptize babies. Priests were thought to be the only middlemen standing between God and humans. And the pope held supreme power within the Church. He and he alone was the final authority on what was or was not true Christian belief.

The Church, then, played an essential part in the spiritual lives of all Christians. But its influence went much further than that. The pope could influence the decisions of kings and other rulers. And good Christians paid one tenth of their yearly income to the Church. Even less devout Christians were constantly reminded of their Church. Church bells woke them up in the morning. Holidays were "holy days," set by the Church.

Questions Arise. Yet by 1500 some Christians regarded the Church with uneasiness. Wars, famines, and diseases such as the bubonic plague made death a familiar visitor to most families. People worried about whether they would go to heaven after they died. Was it enough for them to go to church regularly and receive the sacraments?

Many Christians tried to be as religious as possible. They prayed for hours and fasted for days. They tried to be generous to the poor and sick. Some obeyed the writings of Thomas à Kempis. His book,

The Imitation of Christ, advised Christians to avoid all worldly pleasures. People, Kempis wrote, were naturally sinful. They could only be saved by loving Jesus Christ.

However, while ordinary people tried to live piously, the clergy often did not. Seeds of corruption and disorder were sown in the Church in the late Middle Ages and flowered in the Renaissance. Some priests and bishops had stopped taking their religion seriously. They did not always follow Church law. Sometimes they took Church money for their own use. Many of them made deals with princes and kings.

Even some popes became deeply involved in politics. They lived lavishly while peasants starved to pay Church taxes. Some priests and a few popes even fathered children, though it was strictly forbidden.

Therefore, many Christians believed that the Church had become too wealthy and powerful for its own good. It had wandered away from the ideals of Jesus. In the view of many Europeans, the Church had lost sight of its main aim— the teaching of the Christian faith.

The Beginnings of Change. Long before the sixteenth century, a number of clergy members had made efforts at reform. One of the first was a thirteenth-century Spanish priest named Dominic (DAHM-uh-nick). Early in his priesthood, Dominic preached against *heresy* (HER-uh-see), or the holding of beliefs which differed from Church law. But he did not merely condemn heresy. He tried to understand the people who were guilty of it — heretics (HER-uh-ticks). He decided that many incorrect beliefs had come from priests.

Dominic concluded that priests were not well enough educated. He decided to devote himself to the training of the clergy. He set up an order of monks, called Dominicans (duh-MIN-uh-kins), devoted to religious education. His efforts were so successful that many of the greatest Church thinkers of later years were Dominicans.

Many other reformers helped improve the Church. But their reforms did not put an end to heresy. Some Catholic leaders tried to persuade heretics to change their minds. But others put heretics on trial before a court known as the Inquisition.

The Inquisition started in the early thirteenth century. It was strongest in northern Italy, southern France, and northern Spain (see Chapter 11). If a court found a person guilty of heresy, it would often excommunicate that person, depriving him or her of membership in the Church. In many cases, heretics were

turned over to local officials and burned at the stake.

Such practices may have discouraged some Church reformers. But they did not put an end to all efforts at reform. Many medieval men and women took religion very seriously, and reformers kept on trying to change the Church despite the risks.

Early Reformers. One fourteenth-century reformer was an Englishman named John Wycliffe (WICK-liff). Wycliffe was a professor of religion and thought of himself as a loyal Roman Catholic. Yet he was very troubled by the power of the Church. He objected to the Church's claim that it alone could interpret the meaning of the Bible for the people.

Wycliffe believed that salvation was to be obtained from God directly. In his view, the Church was not necessary as a go-between. Despite the protests of the clergy, Wycliffe had the Bible translated from Latin into English. He hoped to make the scriptures available to every Christian who could read.

Wycliffe's ideas soon spread beyond England. They were picked up by John Huss, a Roman Catholic priest from Bohemia (bo-HEE-mee-uh; now part of

Reformer John Huss (bottom), a student of Wycliffe (above), was burned at the stake by the Catholic Church, as was Savanarola (left). Page 124: Catholic procession in St. Mark's square, Venice.

Czechoslovakia). Like Wycliffe, Huss preached against the wealth and power of the Church. In 1415 he was burned at the stake as a heretic. But his ideas lived on to influence later Christian reformers.

Attacks on Church authority deeply troubled many Christians. These people wanted the Church to remain as united as it could. Yet the tide was moving in a different direction. Now other groups were arising to challenge the power of the Church in Europe.

One challenge came from Europe's peasants. They wanted more freedom from their rulers. The peasants objected whenever the Church acted in their rulers' behalf. Another challenge came from the rising merchant class. They were angered by Church laws preventing the lending of money at interest. Some members of the nobility also opposed the Church. They envied the Church's money and land. Partly for that reason, they objected to having to send their own tax money to Rome.

By 1500, then, the Church was the object of many grievances. Though the Church still commanded the loyalty of most Europeans, it had many critics. Thus, the stage was set for a dramatic reform movement—one that would take its followers completely outside the Church.

129

18
Ninety-Five Theses

Martin Luther of Germany was the person most responsible for the reform movement called the Reformation. He was born in 1483. When he was a young man, he wanted to become a lawyer. But one night, as the story goes, he was caught in a thunderstorm. A bolt of lightning hit him and knocked him to the ground. Terrified, he promised God that he would become a monk if he lived through the storm.

Luther lived. As a monk, he spent most of his time thinking about religion and about the Church. He studied hard and became a professor of religion. All the while, he tried desperately to sort out his ideas about religion. He was convinced that he had committed many sins. The Church taught him that he could get

to heaven if he did good works to make up for his sins. But how could God love such a sinner? Martin Luther wondered. Could he really be admitted to heaven on the basis of his actions alone?

Luther fasted and prayed constantly. Finally he began reading the Bible very carefully. He focused on the words of the apostle Paul, who wrote, "The just shall live by faith alone." Then Luther decided that he could earn God's love by having great faith in God. Luther came to believe that he could not get to heaven simply by lighting candles, praying all the time, or donating money to the Church. Getting into heaven was not a matter of behavior. It was a matter of faith.

Luther might have kept his ideas to himself. However, in 1517 a Dominican

Martin Luther, leader of the Reformation

friar named Johann (YO-hahn) Tetzel came to Luther's part of Germany. Here is how Luther's diary might have told what took place then:

Wittenberg, Saxony,
Holy Roman Empire

November 26, 1519

I still can't believe what's happened! Everything has changed since the day Johann Tetzel came to town selling indulgences, or pardons. People would tell him they had committed a sin, then pay him money. So Tetzel would tell them that God forgave them. He didn't ask if they were sorry, and it didn't matter how serious the sin was. As long as they had money, they were pardoned.

That hasn't always been the practice of the Church. Pardons were ways that people could make up for past or future sins. One way of getting pardons was by giving money for the poor. But pardon-selling began during the Crusades. Now the practice is approved of by our local bishop and the pope in Rome.

In my opinion, the selling of pardons has gone too far. Besides, I don't think God would forgive a sin unless the sinner was really sorry. The whole business of indulgences is bad for the people and bad for the Church.

I thought about what Tetzel was doing. Then I did what any good Christian teacher would do. I challenged Tetzel and others to talk about it. I wrote up a list of things I believed. I said it seemed to me that the best way to get to heaven was to have faith in God and in Christ. I said I didn't think you could buy your way into heaven. In all, my list had 95 theses, or statements, in it. I nailed my list up on the church door.

But I didn't realize what a big fuss there would be! Someone took my list and printed it. Before I knew it, every town in Germany was reading what I wrote. Johann Tetzel was heckled and thrown out of the country.

I thought the fuss would die down. But people just wouldn't stop talking about my list. They kept arguing about my ideas, and that made me think even more. I went back to the Bible and read more and more. Now I've reached some new conclusions about my faith.

I think the Church has made many mistakes. I think it has forgotten some of the things Jesus taught us. I agree that human beings are sinful by nature. But I don't believe any of us can get into heaven by buying indulgences or even by praying. According to the Bible, faith is the most important thing for a Christian. It's more important than Church ceremonies and building expensive cathedrals. It's more important than how priests live or if they get married.

The pope has tried to get me to say I'm mistaken. But I won't unless someone can show me in the Bible that I'm wrong. I'm sorry I have to disagree with my Church, but I'm convinced I'm right. So I'm going to keep on teaching and writing. I want all Christians everywhere to know the truth.

Pope Leo, who excommunicated Luther, flanked by two cardinals

In 1521 the pope excommunicated Luther. And the Holy Roman Emperor, Charles V, declared him an outlaw. Charles was one of the most powerful men in Europe. Besides being the Holy Roman Emperor, he was the king of Spain. He was a very devout Roman Catholic, and he thought Luther's ideas were dangerous.

Later during the same year, Luther was brought before Charles V and many prominent Catholics at Worms, Germany. Charles asked Luther if he would *recant*, or take back, the heretical statements in his books. Luther refused. He said that he could not go against his conscience unless convinced to do so by the Bible or by reason. The angry emperor dismissed Luther. Then he issued the Edict of Worms, which branded Luther an outlaw. It also banned all of Luther's writings.

The Prince of Saxony liked Luther and gave him a safe haven in his castle for a year. During that time, Luther translated the entire New Testament from Greek to German. In 1522 he began preaching again.

The pope and Charles V would have liked to get rid of Luther. But much of Germany was ruled by regional princes. Many of them defended Luther and fought back against Charles V. This led to a bloody civil war. Large numbers of people were killed on both sides.

The Faith Spreads. But Luther was able to live out his life in peace. He spent his time preaching his views. And his ideas caught on. Soon people in many parts of Europe, but especially in Germany, called themselves Lutherans.

Why did Luther's ideas catch on so quickly? There were several reasons for their success. Some Europeans were already challenging the Church. Some of them were convinced of Luther's teachings. Others were simply tired of paying tax money to Rome.

Lutheranism also spread quickly because some of its rituals were the same as Catholic rituals. For example, Luther believed in transubstantiation and baptism because they were described in the Bible. Preserving these rituals reassured former Catholics. It made their conversion to Lutheranism easier.

133

Even so, Lutheranism might not have become so popular. But just before Luther was born, an important invention had been made. That invention was the printing press. The main credit for this is usually given to a German silversmith named Johann Gutenberg (GOOT-un-burg). Before the printing press, books had to be copied by hand. This took a long time, and very few copies were made. But the printing press made it possible to print many books quickly and cheaply.

Martin Luther's movement depended on books. In Luther's view, people could increase their faith by learning what was in the Bible. But to do that they must be able to read it. Before Luther's time, most books were written in Latin, the language of the clergy. By the time of his death, Luther had translated the entire Bible into German. In this way, he gave his followers a powerful motive for learning how to read.

When he started out, Martin Luther considered himself a good Roman Catholic. Before he died in 1546, however, he knew he had started a new church. His church was different from the Roman Catholic Church in many ways. Members of both churches thought theirs was the only true faith.

In 1555, the civil war sparked by Luther's ideas finally ended. Charles V signed the Peace of Augsburg (OGZ-burg). It said that each ruler could decide whether to be a Roman Catholic or a Lutheran. The ruler's religion became the religion of the people, too.

For the first time, there were two legal Christian churches. And for a while, at least, religious peace came to Germany.

✎ Quick Check

1. Who was Martin Luther? What was he responsible for?

2. Describe Luther's life as a monk. What Church belief disturbed him? What new idea did he have about this?

3. What did Johann Tetzel sell? What did Luther do about it? How did people react?

4. What happened to Luther in 1521? Why? What was the Edict of Worms and how did it affect Luther?

5. Give two reasons why Luther's ideas caught on so quickly. How did the printing press contribute to the spread of Lutheranism?

Printing involved setting type, working the press, and stacking printed sheets.

134

19
The Protest Spreads

Martin Luther's Ninety-five Theses were just the beginning of the Reformation. Soon more and more people were becoming Protestants. They were called Protestants because they protested against things they didn't like in the Roman Catholic Church.

In Switzerland, one of the first Protestants was named Ulrich Zwingli (TZVIN-glee). Zwingli started out as a Roman Catholic priest, but he believed many of the same things Luther did. Finally, Zwingli broke away from the Church. He started his own kind of Christianity in the town of Zurich (ZOOR-ick). His religious ideas were stricter than Luther's. Zwingli even banned the singing of hymns. He slowly turned Zurich into a Protestant center. And he paved the way for another Protestant leader.

This leader was John Calvin. He was a French law student, more interested in religion than in law. He agreed with Luther that what the Bible said was more important than what the Church taught. But he didn't agree with either Luther or the Roman Catholic Church about how to get to heaven.

Calvin believed that people could not get to heaven by their own faith or actions. He thought that God had determined who would be saved even before time began. This belief of Calvin's was called *predestination*. Calvin claimed that it was pointless for people to worry about whether or not they would be saved. God, Calvin felt, had already decided.

Fearing arrest for his ideas, Calvin left France in 1534. He went to Basel, Switzerland, where he published a book of his beliefs two years later. In 1536, while on a journey to a French border town, he stopped for a night in the Swiss city of Geneva. He remained there for most of the rest of his life.

A Christian Society. In Geneva, Calvin gained more and more political power. He also gained followers, who were called Calvinists. In time, Calvinists came to control the Geneva town council. Geneva was run as a stern Christian society. In Calvin's opinion, Christians should behave according to God's will. They should devote themselves to building a prosperous, virtuous community. That is what made Calvinists such serious people.

In some ways, Calvin's rules for living seem very harsh today. Yet Calvinism did allow its members to help run church affairs. Calvinism also stressed the importance of education. As a result, many Protestant scholars from other parts of Europe came to Geneva to study. Other people who believed in Calvin's ideas moved their families to Geneva. They knew that they would be safe there if they followed Calvin's teachings.

If they didn't follow his teachings, they might be executed for heresy. In four years of Calvin's rule, 58 heretics were executed. With only 16,000 people living in Geneva at the time, the number was considerable.

What was life like in Calvin's Geneva?

The time: 1541

John Calvin

The place: the house of Johann, a Genevan carpenter.

The action: Johann is talking to his cousin Max. Max is interested in moving to Geneva.

JOHANN: I am very pleased that you are thinking of moving your family here. Good, God-fearing Christians are always welcome in Geneva.

MAX: My family and I always try to follow Calvin's teachings. But I hear that will be easy to do here. Do you really enforce his beliefs as law?

JOHANN: We certainly do. Just last week, Fritz the shoemaker was caught going to a gypsy to have his fortune read! He wanted to find out whether he would go to heaven. As you know, that is a sin. God has decided our fates, and we cannot know or question them. Well, the authorities threw Fritz into jail.

TEMPLE DE LYON, NOMME PARADIS.

French Huguenot temple at Lyons shows their belief in simplicity. Its rough benches and sparse decor were very different from the ornate interiors of Catholic cathedrals and churches.

MAX: That may be a good thing. After all, if he sins once, what is to stop him from sinning again? We can't have him setting a bad example for our children.

JOHANN: Exactly. The next thing you know, he'd be wanting to dance. Or play cards, or drink beer.

MAX: Or miss the Sunday service. When we move here, I will make sure that my family attends church every Sunday.

JOHANN: By the way, I think you should speak to your wife about her clothes. That red kerchief she wore yesterday may be acceptable where you lived, but it would not be here. We do not approve of bright colors for men either.

In their zeal, Reformers damaged or even destroyed Catholic churches.

MAX: I'll tell her tonight. Well, I must be going. It's almost eight o'clock. The innkeeper told me that we must be in bed by nine. I'm planning on reading his Bible for an hour before bed.

JOHANN: Besides, I have to get up at dawn to work. You will too, once you move here. As it says in the Bible, idleness is a sin, except on Sunday.

Slowly, Calvin's ideas began to spread through Europe. In France, his followers were known as Huguenots (HUE-geh-nots). In Scotland, a Calvinist named John Knox began to spread the new religion. There it came to be known as Presbyterianism (prez-beh-TEHR-ee-uh-niz-um) Everywhere business was growing. Calvinism grew too. One reason for this was that Calvinism taught that a person's work is part of his or her religious life.

By the middle of the sixteenth century, Calvinism and Lutheranism had many followers all over Europe. But they were not the only new Protestant sects. There was a Reformation taking place in England as well.

✎ Quick Check

1. *Who were the Protestants? Who was John Calvin?*

2. *According to Calvin, how did people get to heaven? What is this belief called?*

3. *Why did Calvin go to Switzerland? In what city did he settle? How was this city run? What was life there like? Why?*

4. *Give three examples of how Max and Johann followed Calvin's teachings.*

20
The Act of Supremacy

In Germany and Switzerland, the Reformation was mostly brought about by people with strong religious ideas. In England it occurred in a somewhat different way. Some English people learned of Martin Luther's ideas by as early as 1517. But it took an English king to draw his people away from the Roman Catholic Church.

The English expected great things of Henry VIII from the time he took the throne in 1509. Certainly he was a lively and intelligent king. He hunted, he danced, he played tennis—all with zest. He was also an able student. But he rarely allowed his studies to get in the way of political affairs.

Henry was a complicated man. He could be very charming. Yet he was also a little shy. His temper was quick and furious, and he used it on anyone who made him angry. In his early years he had developed an interest in his Catholic faith. He even wrote a pamphlet against Martin Luther and his ideas.

Very soon after Henry became king, he married a woman five years older than he was. She was Catherine of Aragon, daughter of Ferdinand and Isabella, the king and queen of Spain (see Chapter 11). Catherine had been married to Henry's older brother Arthur, but Arthur died soon after their marriage. Church law forbade a man to marry his brother's widow. But Henry wanted to marry Catherine as a way of improving relations between England and Spain. So he asked Pope Julius II to make an exception to Church law. He wanted the pope to allow them to marry. The pope agreed.

Left, Henry VIII painted by Holbein. His first wife Catherine of Aragon (above).

An Unhappy Marriage. Henry and Catherine were wed. For more than 10 years they seemed happy. Catherine was a quiet and obedient wife, even after Henry began to neglect her. Then, in the late 1520's, trouble set in. The alliance between Spain and England was becoming less popular. Catherine was growing more religious with every passing year. And in 1527 Henry fell in love with a beautiful lady-in-waiting, Anne Boleyn (buh-LINN).

Anne was just twenty, but very ambitious. She had no interest in a brief love affair, and ignored the king's attentions. But the more she ignored him, the more he loved her. Finally she said that she could return his affection if he married her and made her queen of England.

Each of these things put a strain on Henry's marriage. But each was minor compared to the greatest problem of all. The royal couple had not produced a son who could serve as heir to the English throne. All but one of their children had died in infancy. The only survivor was a daughter, Mary.

Henry blamed Catherine for their failure to have a son. He began looking for a way to put an end to his marriage. Henry planned to marry Anne Boleyn, hoping that she would bear him a male heir. So in 1527 Henry began claiming that he was living in sin because he had married his brother's widow.

A Clash with the Pope. Ending Henry's marriage turned out to be more difficult than entering it. According to the Church, marriages were supposed to last forever. Divorce was not permitted. So Henry asked that his marriage be annulled (declared never to have existed) by the pope. Henry argued that it had been illegal all along.

Had it? The question hinged on the fact that Pope Julius II had allowed the marriage. To end the marriage, the current pope, Clement, would have to rule that Julius II had made an error. Pope Clement might have done so. But Catherine of Aragon warned him against it.

Catherine was protesting Henry's plan

141

to annul their marriage. She was determined to remain queen. She also meant to keep her daughter Mary as the only heir to the throne. Henry was astonished by her pride and stubbornness.

Henry might have been able to defeat Catherine and the pope easily. But the queen had strong backing from her nephew Charles V, the Holy Roman Emperor. Charles was very powerful, and his army had already attacked Rome in 1527. The pope feared Charles, and so he tried to put off a decision on Henry's request. The delay made things worse.

Henry had long ago grown used to getting his way most of the time. Now he knew what he wanted, and that was to get out of his marriage. It seemed to him that he was being trapped in it, and in mortal sin, by the pope. Under Anne Boleyn's prodding, Henry grew more and more impatient to marry her. By early 1530, he had begun to look for ways to cut down the power of the pope in England.

In that year, he threatened the English clergy with a heavy fine unless they recognized him as head of the Church in England. The clergy agreed. Then, in 1532, Henry had Parliament pass a law allowing him to cut off part of the taxes owed to Rome if the pope did not grant the divorce. The next year Henry had his own archbishop give him a divorce from Catherine. In May of 1533, Anne Boleyn became queen.

Henry still hoped that the pope would bless his second marriage. Instead, the

Henry's marriage to Anne Boleyn led to the formation of the Church of England.

pope excommunicated the English king. In 1534 Henry took revenge. He had Parliament enact two laws. One made his divorce legal. The other went much farther.

The New Church. The second law was called the Act of Supremacy. It set up the Church of England (also known as the Anglican Church). The church was to be a national one, and foreigners were not to interfere with it. It would be headed by the king of England, not the pope in Rome.

Having broken with the pope, Henry went one step further. Guided partly by greed, he persuaded Parliament to close all of England's monasteries. The process

Jane Seymour (bottom), Henry's third wife, gave birth to Edward VI (top).

took place in two stages. The smaller monasteries were closed in 1536. The larger ones were closed in 1539. Then the Church lands were seized and sold at market prices.

Henry also made some minor changes in church services. He allowed the publication of a Bible which had been translated into English. But he did not make basic changes in religious belief. Anglicans still held many Catholic beliefs. Their habits of worship were largely Catholic, too. Henry did not think of himself as a Protestant. He had created the Church of England primarily to end the pope's involvement in English affairs. His reasons for changing the Church were personal and political, not spiritual.

Yet Henry's actions opened the way for the Protestant Reformation in England. Over the next 50 years, the ideas of Luther and Calvin spread among the English people.

A Woman Rules. To Henry's disappointment, Anne Boleyn bore only one child—a daughter, Elizabeth. This strained their relationship. When Anne was accused of adultery, Henry readily took action. He shut Anne up in the Tower of London, where political prisoners were kept. Then he ordered her executed. It was a convenient way out of an unsatisfying marriage. It also left Henry free to marry again.

Eleven days later, Henry married Jane Seymour, another lady-in-waiting. Soon she bore a son, Edward, and died. Henry

143

went on to marry three more women, but Edward was his last child.

The boy became King Edward VI on his father's death in 1547. Under Edward's reign, the Church of England actually became Protestant. So did many members of England's ruling classes. But the young king died after only six years on the throne.

The crown went to his older sister, Mary (Henry's daughter by Catherine of Aragon). Mary had never forgotten her mother's unhappy marriage. Also, she thought of herself as a devout Catholic. Once she took the throne, she attempted to wipe out many of the changes her father had made. Hundreds of Protestants were tortured and burned at the stake. Thus, Mary came to be nicknamed "Bloody Mary."

When Mary died in 1558, her half-sister Elizabeth became queen. In his efforts to produce a male heir, Henry never dreamed that Elizabeth would become one of England's greatest monarchs. But Elizabeth was far more tolerant than her sister Mary. Although she was a Protestant, she had no wish to offend English Catholics.

In her efforts to bring England back to Catholicism, Mary I (bottom) had some 300 Protestants put to death.

✎ Quick Check

1. *Who was Henry VIII's first wife? What four things put a strain on their marriage?*

2. *Why did Henry clash with the pope? What did he do to cut down the power of the pope in 1530? In 1532?*

3. *Who finally granted Henry's divorce? How did the pope react?*

4. *What was the Act of Supremacy? Why was it enacted? How did the Anglican Church differ from the Catholic Church? How were the two churches similar?*

5. *Who was "Bloody Mary"? How did she earn this name? Who became queen after Mary?*

21
The Soldier of God

By the middle of the sixteenth century, there were Protestants in most countries of Europe. Roman Catholic leaders wanted to try to win some of them back. Many Catholics also felt that some changes were needed within the Church. In other words, they wanted to strengthen the Roman Catholic Church by reforming it.

Out of this unrest came a new movement. It was later called the Catholic Reformation, or Counter-Reformation. One leader of this movement was a Spaniard with a deep devotion to the Church.

One night in 1521 a handsome young soldier lay on a battlefield in Spain. He had been fighting for his town against the French. His legs had been smashed by cannonballs. As he lay there, he thought he might die.

This young man was later called Ignatius (ig-NAY-shuss) of Loyola (loy-OH-lah). He nearly died, but was given medical care and saved. His recovery was slow and painful. While his legs were healing, Loyola decided to give the rest of his life to God. He had been a soldier for his country. Now he would be a soldier for his Church.

But becoming a soldier of God wasn't easy. Loyola realized that he didn't know very much about the Church. So he started training himself. He prayed as much as seven hours a day. He visited as many holy places as he could. And then he set out on almost 15 years of study.

Loyola was in his thirties when he entered school in the Spanish city of Barcelona (bar-seh-LOW-nuh). There he learned Latin with boys half his age. After two years in Barcelona, he attended other schools in Spain and in Paris. He studied art, science, and most of all, religion.

Recruits for the Church. While in Paris, he drew together his first religious followers. In 1534 the members of this group pledged to devote themselves to the Church. They made plans to go to Rome and serve the pope.

In 1537 Loyola became a priest. Three years later the pope approved the formation of Loyola's new order. It would be called the Society of Jesus. Its members would be known as Jesuits (JEZ-wuts), and Loyola would be the leader.

This new order was quite different from all others in the Church. It was organized like an army. Each "soldier" had to go through long schooling, just as Loyola had. Each had to obey the person in charge of him, without question.

As Loyola saw it, the Church needed "soldiers" to fight off its main enemy—the Protestant Reformation. He believed that one weakness in Protestantism was that there was no single person in charge. So he stressed that Roman Catholicism had such a person — the pope.

Loyola carried on his battle by preaching. His well-trained Jesuits had a gift for winning people over to their beliefs. They not only did so in Europe. They traveled to distant lands such as Africa, America, and East Asia, and converted many people to Christianity.

Perhaps Loyola's greatest success was in education. From the first, he wanted

Pope Paul III received Loyola in 1540. Loyola was canonized after his death.

Jesuits to be scholars. In the last 15 years of his life, he set up dozens of schools to train his priests. As more and more Jesuits became teachers, their fame grew. Within a century, a number of Jesuits were being invited to head schools.

Slowing the Reformation. Loyola died in Rome in 1556. He had not fought for his country since that night on the battlefield in 1521. But he had kept on fighting for his Roman Catholic faith. And his priests had slowed the spread of Protestant reform.

Roman Catholics did other things to try to stop the Protestant Reformation. The pope decided to make the Inquisition stronger. And the Church published a list of books, called the *Index*. Good Roman Catholics were not supposed to read books on the *Index*. Many of these books were written by Protestants.

In 1545 the pope opened a meeting of religious leaders and thinkers. It was called the Council of Trent after the south German town in which it was held. The council was supposed to look at Church laws and decide which of them needed changing. It did away with some practices of the mass service which had been criticized by both Protestants and Roman Catholic reformers. It also urged the clergy to reform. Finally, it labeled the Protestant movement heresy.

On the whole, the Counter-Reformation was successful. For one thing, it got people interested in the Roman Catholic Church again. For another, it changed some things that many Christians thought were wrong with that Church. In the end, the Church emerged more centralized and even stricter in its beliefs than it had been in the Middle Ages.

✎ **Quick Check**

1. What was the purpose of the Counter-Reformation?

2. Why was Loyola devoted to the Church? How did he train himself to become a soldier of God?

3. What order did Loyola form? What was its purpose and how did it operate? What was its greatest success?

4. What was the Index? *What was the Council of Trent? What three things did it do?*

The Council of Trent, shown in session, met to reform Church laws and practices.

RELIGION IN EUROPE

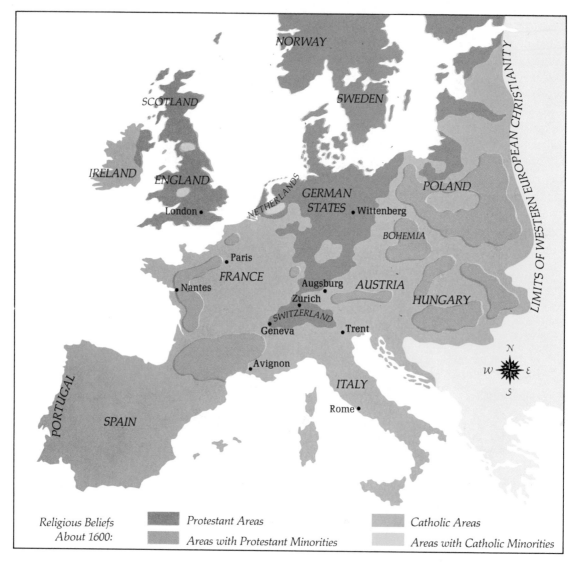

Religious Beliefs About 1600:
Protestant Areas
Areas with Protestant Minorities
Catholic Areas
Areas with Catholic Minorities

MAP EXERCISE

This map shows Protestant and Catholic areas in Europe in about 1600. Use the map to answer the following questions.

1. According to the map, what kind of Christianity was dominant in northern Europe in 1600? In southern Europe?

2. Name a city in the western part of France with a Protestant minority.

3. Name two areas that had Catholic minorities.

4. What form of Christianity would a person living in Rome probably have practiced in 1600? In London?

22
Christians Against Christians

In northern Europe, the Reformation was a powerful movement. The ideas of Martin Luther led to a bloody conflict among German rulers and their followers. But northern Europe was not the only area to be caught up in religious wars. France was also a battleground. There the Reformation met its first major setback.

In France the call for Protestant reform was first sounded in the 1520's. French Calvinists were called Huguenots (HUE-geh-nots). But the French king, Francis I, did not encourage the Huguenot movement in his country. The more the movement grew in France, the more it came to be feared and hated by many French Catholics. This was the reason why John Calvin fled to Switzerland in 1534 (see Chapter 19).

Little by little, French Huguenots grew more daring. In 1560 a group of them plotted to kill some of the king's counselors. The plan was uncovered, and the leaders of the plot were caught. The king's counselors were outraged. They crushed the revolt with such force that they touched off a civil war.

The fighting raged on and off from 1562 to 1598. Religious quarrels played a part in it. But they were not the only cause of the war. Much of the fighting was waged by one faction or another for control of the French government. Even so, the conflict has gone down in history as the Wars of Religion.

In time, many French people wearied of the fighting. They saw the need for greater moderation in French affairs. One famous writer, Michel de Montaigne (me-SHELL duh mahn-TANE), put this thought into one of his essays: Do we not value our own opinions too highly, he asked, when we "roast people alive" for disagreeing with us?

The Conflict Continues. France needed a leader who would unite all the French people. In 1589 it finally got one of the strongest leaders of the age.

Henry of Navarre (nuh-VAHR) was never meant to be a religious leader. He believed in religious tolerance and moderation. But he loved France more than anything. "We are born not only for ourselves," he once told the French people, "but above all to serve the country."

Henry was born near the French-Spanish border in 1553. When he was still quite young, his father, a Catholic, was killed in a battle against Protestants. But his mother stood firm in her own religious beliefs. Soon after her husband's death, she announced she was a Calvinist. From the time Henry was 13, he was raised in the Protestant faith.

Henry's father had been a French duke. Through him, Henry was an heir to the French throne. When Henry was 18, he became engaged to the French king's sister. The wedding was to be held in Paris in August 1572. Many Protestant nobles gathered in the city to attend.

The wedding took place on schedule. Then, four days later, the city was suddenly bathed in blood. Thousands of Huguenots were murdered in the St. Bartholomew's Day Massacre. Historians are still not sure who planned the attack.

But the main plotter may have been Catherine de Medici, a member of the Medici family of Florence, with her son Henry who would soon be crowned King Henry III.

The massacre made Huguenots very bitter. It deepened the political and religious conflict in France. Henry of Navarre escaped injury, but he was taken prisoner at the court of Henry III. At the king's order, Henry of Navarre agreed to give up his Protestant faith.

He remained the king's captive for the next three and one-half years. In 1576 he escaped. Once free, he went back to being a Huguenot. He defended Protestant churches against a Catholic group called the Holy League. In this fighting, Henry proved to be a gallant military leader. At one point, he captured a town held by the League without firing a single shot.

A New Leader. In August 1589, King Henry III was stabbed by a French monk. As he lay dying, he called Henry of Navarre to his bed. He offered the younger man the French crown and urged him to again change his faith. Henry of Navarre accepted the crown and became King Henry IV. But he did not accept the dying king's advice about changing his faith. He said he would not become a Catholic while a knife was pointed at his throat.

The war between the Protestant Huguenots and the Catholic Holy League continued. Slowly Henry realized that he could end the fighting by becoming a Roman Catholic like most of his country-

In sixteenth-century Europe, politics and religion both played an important part in the murder of Protestants on St. Bartholomew's Day in Paris in 1572.

men. Finally, in 1593, he decided, in his own words, to "jump the ditch." In the town of Saint Denis (SAN duh-NEE) near Paris, he was welcomed into the Catholic faith. He was officially crowned King Henry IV the following February.

The war against the Holy League dragged on fitfully for another four years. But now that Henry was a Catholic, most of the French people accepted him as their king. He moved further toward religious peace while visiting the city of Nantes (nahnt) in western France in 1598.

There Henry issued an official order known as an edict. The Edict of Nantes gave Huguenots freedom to worship in certain places. It gave them the right to be employed by the state. It set up special courts to see that they got justice. In short, it recognized their right to be French and Protestant at the same time.

Trying Out Toleration. In France, Protestants and Roman Catholics had fought their way to a draw. The Protestants had not succeeded in winning over most French people. The Catholics had not succeeded in stamping out the Protestant faith. There was no winner in the struggle, unless it was the French monarchy. The wars had left France badly divided, and now a series of strong French kings created a unity of their own.

The Edict of Nantes did not settle the religious question in France once and for all. In 1685 King Louis XIV revoked (called back) the edict, and more than 250,000 Protestants then fled France. But over a longer period, the edict did suggest one solution to religious warfare. That solution was national unity based on religious toleration.

In many parts of Europe, new Protestant sects kept appearing. Some of them were centered around a leader. Others were centered around a special idea. The Protestant revolt not only split Europe's religious unity, it also contributed to democratic thinking.

Europe would never again be a Catholic Christian community. The Reformation, bringing in many different forms of Protestantism, had changed that. But by the end of the sixteenth century, the general pattern of religious belief had been set. A religious map of Europe in 1600 looks very much like a religious map of Europe today.

✎ **Quick Check**

1. *Who were the Huguenots? How did they help start a civil war in France? How long did the fighting last?*

2. *What was the St. Bartholomew's Day Massacre? Who do historians blame for plotting it? What happened to Henry of Navarre because of the conflict?*

3. *What did Henry do when he "jumped the ditch"? How did the French people react?*

4. *What was the Edict of Nantes? What solution to religious warfare did the Edict suggest?*

Tapestry detail shows Catherine de Medici (right) with Henry of Navarre.

PART 4
Review and Skills Exercises

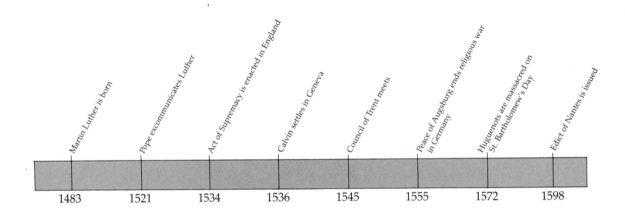

Martin Luther is born · Pope excommunicates Luther · Act of Supremacy is enacted in England · Calvin settles in Geneva · Council of Trent meets · Peace of Augsburg ends religious war in Germany · Huguenots are massacred on St. Bartholomew's Day · Edict of Nantes is issued

1483   1521   1534   1536   1545   1555   1572   1598

Understanding Events

Part 4 covers events of the Reformation. You read about religious conflicts and reformers. Study the time line above and answer the following questions.

1. When was Martin Luther born? How many years after that did the pope excommunicate him?

2. How many years ago was the Act of Supremacy enacted in England?

3. Which event occurred first, the meeting of the Council of Trent or the St. Bartholomew's Day Massacre?

4. When did the Peace of Augsburg end the religious war, before or after Calvin settled in Geneva?

5. In what year was the Edict of Nantes issued? How many years after the St. Bartholomew's Day Massacre was it issued?

Establishing a Point of View

A *point of view* is a person's belief about an issue. Below is a list of people and the issues that concerned them. Choose one of the people and write a short paragraph giving his point of view. Write as if the person you have selected were speaking about the issue next to his name.

1. John Wycliffe—the power of the church
2. Martin Luther—the selling of indulgences

3. Ignatius of Loyola—the reasons he founded a religious order

Building Vocabulary

This exercise has two parts. Part A lists events from the Reformation. Part B lists names of religious groups. Both lists are followed by definitions. For each part, write the numbers 1–8 on a sheet of paper. Then write the letter of the correct definition by each number.

A

1. Inquisition
2. Reformation
3. Edict of Worms
4. Peace of Augsburg
5. Act of Supremacy
6. Counter-Reformation
7. Council of Trent
8. Edict of Nantes

a. the sentence passed on Martin Luther that branded him an outlaw and banned his writings
b. a movement within the Roman Catholic Church to stop Protestantism
c. the Church court that punished heretics, sometimes with death
d. a religious movement that began in the 1500's and led to the establishment of Protestantism
e. a meeting of Catholic leaders and thinkers that changed some practices of the Church
f. the decree by King Henry IV that allowed Huguenots freedom of worship in some places in France
g. an agreement that ended a civil war in 1555 and allowed the rulers of German states to choose between Catholicism and Protestantism
h. a decision made by the English Parliament (under Henry VIII's instructions) that established the Church of England

B

1. Dominicans
2. Lutherans
3. Protestants
4. Calvinists
5. Presbyterians
6. Huguenots
7. Anglicans
8. Jesuits

a. followers of a Protestant movement that began with the teachings of Martin Luther in Germany
b. members of the church of England who split from the Roman Catholic Church in 1534
c. members of a religious order founded by Ignatius of Loyola
d. members of a religious order established by a Spanish monk, Dominic, in the thirteenth century
e. French followers of the teachings of John Calvin
f. a Protestant movement that developed from the teachings of a Frenchman who settled in Switzerland
g. followers of beliefs that developed in the 1500's as a protest against certain practices of the Roman Catholic Church
h. followers in Scotland of the teaching of John Knox, who spread the ideas of John Calvin

PART
5

THE AGE OF DISCOVERY

A red and white striped sail! No sight on the horizon brought more fear to European monks. It meant the Vikings were coming. Soon their long, flat-bottomed ships would pull up on shore. They would put down their oars, grab their swords and wooden shields, and attack. A Viking attack was fearsome. The warriors worked themselves into a frenzy. In this state they felt no fear or pain. Loot, not murder, was their goal. But many monks died, nevertheless.

Monasteries were easy targets. Their gold and ivory artworks and fine tapestries were guarded only by unarmed monks. When they got their loot, the Vikings sailed home to the frozen shores of Scandinavia. No one knew where or when they might strike again. Most of Europe's monasteries were attacked by Vikings at least once between 800 and 1000.

Western Europe was not the only place the Vikings sailed. They were as fearless on the sea as on land, and they ventured far into unknown waters. They sailed across the Atlantic Ocean to Iceland in about 860. Then, about the year 1000, one of them, Leif Eriksson (leaf ERR-ick-son) landed on the North American coast, in what is now called Newfoundland. Finding wild grapes, he named the place Vinland.

Vikings, who were among the earliest European explorers, struck terror in the hearts of many. Page 156: In the late 1200's, Marco Polo traveled to China.

Europeans settled into feudalism, which helped to protect them from Viking attacks. But it did little to promote adventure. Most Europeans were afraid of the Atlantic Ocean. They referred to it as the Sea of Darkness, or the Green Sea

Scandinavians were good at surviving cold weather. Above, they hunt on skis.

of Gloom. From time to time, some Europeans seemed dimly aware that there was land on the other side of the ocean. But only a few of them risked learning more.

Not until the fourteenth century did Europeans really begin trading with Asian people in lands such as China or India. European explorers like Marco Polo had traveled there, mostly overland. European traders followed the same routes. They brought back silks, spices, and other luxuries.

Exploring by Sea. The spirit of the Renaissance encouraged Europeans to look beyond the Old World. Early in the fourteenth century, King Dinis (duh-NEESH) of Portugal decided to build a good navy to promote trade in his kingdom. He turned for help to the Italian city of

Genoa, which was one of the main ports in Europe. He invited a leading Genoese admiral and 20 captains and navigators to Portugal to train its sailors.

Within about a hundred years, the Portuguese navy was the best in all Europe. Within another hundred years, the Portuguese had inspired journeys into the unknown Atlantic Ocean. They had begun the greatest era of exploration the world had seen.

Scientific progress was very important to these early explorations. Ships were growing larger, and new inventions were helping to guide their journeys. Perhaps the most important of these inventions was the compass, which may have come from the Arabs or the Chinese. Before the compass, sailors had to set their course by the sun or stars. With the compass, they could determine their direction on even the cloudiest nights.

Charting the Course. Portugal produced one of the key figures in the history of navigation. He was the youngest son of Portugal's King John I. Later English writers called this man Prince Henry the Navigator. That is how he is known today.

Henry's story began in 1415. In that year Portugal conquered the Moroccan port of Ceuta (SAY-oot-uh). Henry was named governor there. In Ceuta, he

Henry the Navigator improved the compass and methods of shipbuilding. The exploration he encouraged led to Portugal's becoming a colonial empire.

heard travelers tell marvelous stories of an African country south of the Sahara Desert. They described a lush land with great rivers. There was said to be plenty of gold and ivory there.

After some months in Morocco, Henry returned home. But the tales about Africa had sparked his interest in exploration. Henry wanted to increase Portuguese power and spread the Christian faith. He must also have known that success would bring his country greater wealth. And so, like King Dinis, he focused his attention on the sea.

In 1419 Henry was made governor of Portugal's southernmost province. He started a small court at Sagres (SAHG-reesh), a rocky point of land at Portugal's southwestern tip. At Sagres he built a palace and observatory. At the nearby town of Lagos (LAH-goss) he built docks and shipyards.

At Sagres, Henry was joined by shipbuilders, navigators, and mapmakers. Under Henry's direction, they pooled their knowledge of the sea. Carefully, they studied travelers' reports and accounts of early voyages. Out of their efforts came better ships, finer maps, and more reliable instruments. With improved equipment, they could plan more daring voyages.

Henry was the chief planner. His role was to encourage other sailors—to drive them on, if necessary. From Sagres, Portuguese ships sailed out into the dangerous Atlantic. Soon, Portuguese sailors captured the Azores (AY-zores) to the west of Portugal. They captured Madeira (muh-DIR-uh) to the south. Sugar and other products from these islands paid for new voyages.

The early conquests were the easy ones. Henry had a harder time persuading sailors to go south along Africa's Atlantic coast. Navigators were discouraged by the great westward bulge of the African continent. They reported that the African coast was so barren that no European could live there. They said the sea was so thick with salt that no ship could plow through it.

Urging Sailors South. While his captains warned against such voyages, Henry urged the sailors even more. At last he persuaded them to try. In time, they found their way south. In the 1440's they passed Cape Blanco. They reached the "land of wealth," Africa's Gold Coast. They traded European goods there for gold and ivory. This helped pay for more voyages.

Not all of their trade was in gold or ivory, however. Some of it was cruel, especially the trade in African slaves. This trade had been carried on by Arabs since the eleventh century. Now the Portuguese became involved. By 1448 the trade in slaves had become large enough for Henry to open the first European trading post in Africa.

But the slave trade was only one purpose of the Portuguese voyages. In Henry's time, the main purpose was exploration and the wealth that it might bring. As time went on, these voyages put a new idea in some sailors' minds. They hoped to reach Asia by rounding Africa's southern coast.

Henry died in 1460 without ever having taken one of his own voyages of discovery. He had sailed no foreign seas. He had sighted no new lands. But his vision and will had encouraged others. He, more than anyone, influenced the great explorers.

23
Admiral of the Ocean Sea

By 1460 Prince Henry's seamen had sailed more than a third of the way across the Atlantic Ocean. They had traveled south more than 1,500 miles. But it was not until 28 years after Henry's death that a Portuguese captain made the most important trip. In 1488 Bartholomew Diaz (DEE-ash) reached the southern tip of Africa. He proved that there was an all-water route to East Asia.

His discovery was a triumph for the Portuguese. But it disappointed a 37-year-old Genoese sailor named Christopher Columbus. He had come to Portugal in 1488 with a different plan.

Christopher Columbus had first explained his idea to the Portuguese in 1484. He called his plan the "Enterprise of the Indies." The plan was simple and startling at the same time. Columbus believed, as did most educated Europeans,

that the world was round. If so, he argued, there was no need to sail south around the tip of Africa to reach East Asia. All one had to do was sail *west*—across the Atlantic.

Columbus did not simply argue that such a voyage was possible. He actually thought it would be shorter than the trip around the southern edge of Africa. He estimated the distance between the Canary Islands and the coast of China to be 3,550 nautical miles. That was several hundred miles less than the distance between the Cape Verde Islands and Africa's southern tip (see map p. 169).

Columbus had, of course, made two huge errors. First, the actual distance between the Canary Islands and the Chinese coast is about 11,700 miles. Second, the trip cannot be made in a direct line by sea. Two vast continents stand in

Christopher Columbus believed that God had singled him out for greatness.

162

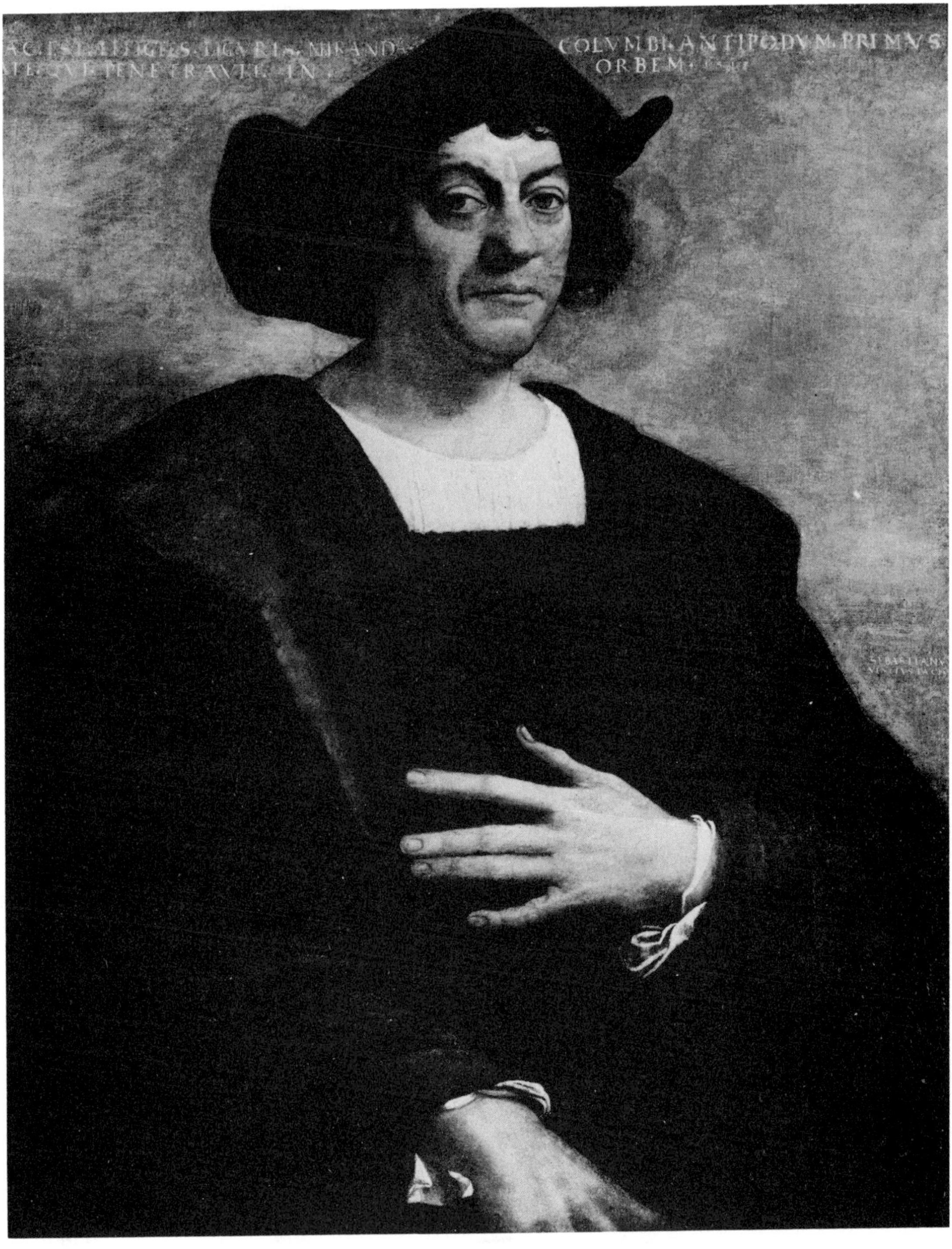
COLVMBI ANTIPODVM PRIMVS
ORBEM

the way—North and South America. Columbus never dreamed they existed.

What was so startling about Columbus's plan? It was neither his arithmetic nor his logic. His suggestion that ships could reach the East by sailing west wasn't surprising, either. The Greek thinker Aristotle (AR-uh-stot-ul) had probably suggested that idea 1,800 years earlier. Even some Europeans had discussed it much more recently than that.

What was startling about Columbus's plan was his determination to make such a voyage himself. Columbus was a devout Christian, and he believed that God had selected him for the task. It did not matter to Columbus that he had never commanded a ship at sea. He had plenty of seafaring experience to guide him.

Searching for Support. But first he needed backing. He needed ships, equipment and a crew. He tried to get such backing from the Portuguese. Then he asked for backing from Queen Isabella of Spain. Then he asked the Portuguese again. But in 1488 the Diaz voyage gave Portugal an all-water route to the riches of the East. The Portuguese did not need or want another one. So Columbus went back to Isabella once more. She had listened to his plan seriously, and now she was his greatest hope.

Isabella had at least two reasons for backing Columbus. First, she envied Portugal's success at sea and wanted similar success for Spain. Second, she was a devout Christian. She saw in Columbus's plan a way of competing with the spread

Queen Isabella of Spain

of Islam by getting new territory. Yet she had already committed most of her money and energy to driving the Moors from Spain (see Chapter 11).

So Columbus waited. He followed Isabella and her court on many of their travels. All along, he hoped that the queen would see him again. Then, early in 1492, he learned that the queen had finally turned down his idea. Furious, he left the Spanish court and headed for France.

Just then, one of the queen's attendants argued Columbus's case to her. This courtier predicted that the plan would bring Isabella great gains for very little risk. He also said that he could raise some of the money for the trip. This time the queen agreed, and Columbus returned to her court. He was to be granted the titles he wanted: "Viceroy of the Indies" and "Admiral of the Ocean Sea." At this time much of the Atlantic was known as the Ocean Sea.

The Voyage East. In the spring of 1492, Columbus's "Enterprise of the Indies" got under way. Columbus located three ships. They were the flagship, the *Santa Maria*, and two smaller vessels, the *Pinta* and the *Niña*. By midsummer he had gathered a crew of 90 men and stocked the ships with food. Shortly before dawn on August 3, 1492, the small fleet sailed from Palos, Spain. It stopped briefly at the Canary Islands off the coast of Africa. Then, on September 9, the voyage began. It was a voyage that would change the world.

Crossing the Atlantic took 33 days. The three small ships had clear sailing all the way. But as the crew traveled farther into uncharted waters, they became more restless. Twice, sailors thought they spotted land. Both times their sightings turned out to be false. Near the end of the crossing, there were open threats of mutiny on the ships.

Then, on October 11, sticks, branches, and land plants appeared in the water. At 10 o'clock that evening Columbus thought he saw a distant light. Four hours later a lookout on the *Pinta* spotted a sand cliff—or something like it. The cry went up in Spanish. *"Tierra!"* ("Land!") The *Niña, Pinta,* and *Santa Maria* had arrived in the New World.

The land they were approaching was one of the Bahama Islands—probably the one called Watling Island today. But Columbus thought he had reached the Indies, the islands to the south of Asia. He went ashore on October 12 and claimed the island in the name of Ferdinand and Isabella. He named the island San Salvador. He called the people he met there Indians.

Having reached what he thought were the Indies, Columbus assumed that Japan could not be far away. From Japan, it would be only a short distance to China. Columbus now set out in search of both places by sailing around the Caribbean Sea. Instead of Japan or China, however, he found two large islands. They were Cuba and Hispaniola (his-pan-YO-luh). (Hispaniola is the island now occupied by Haiti and the Dominican Republic.)

At Hispaniola, the *Santa Maria* ran aground. Columbus abandoned the ship. He left a colony of 38 crew members on the island, and set sail for home. With him he took six Indian captives to be baptized in the Christian faith. He also took the hope that the lands he had "discovered" might yield gold.

On March 15, 1493, the *Niña* sailed truimphantly into Palos harbor in Spain. From there, Columbus traveled to Barcelona to be welcomed by Ferdinand and Isabella. They celebrated his achievement with a mass in the royal chapel. Columbus had reached the high point of his career.

Indians on Hispaniola attack in an attempt to drive back the invading Spanish explorers.

But his career was far from over. Columbus returned to the Americas three more times. On his third voyage, he reached the mouth of the Orinoco (ore-uh-NOH-koh) River at the eastern edge of South America. He decided that the Orinoco must be a great river of Asia. Then he returned to Hispaniola, failing to explore the area.

Columbus died at the age of 54, still thinking that he had found a way to East Asia. It never occurred to him that land stood in the way. Partly for this reason, history played a cruel trick on him. The Americas were not named after Columbus but after an Italian seaman, Amerigo Vespucci (ahm-uh-REE-go veh-SPEW-chee). Vespucci was one of the first to claim that the "Asia" Columbus had found was not Asia, but a new land.

✎ Quick Check

1. *What was Christopher Columbus's plan? What was so startling about it? What were the errors in the plan?*

2. *Who refused to back Columbus? Why? Who gave him support? Why?*

3. *How long did it take Columbus to cross the Atlantic? Where did Columbus think he was when he first sighted land? What islands had he actually discovered?*

4. *For whom were the Americas named? What did this explorer claim about Columbus's discoveries?*

24
Three Sailors

Columbus's first voyage led to greater rivalry between Spain and Portugal. The pope had already given Portugal all the territory from Cape Bojador (BAJ-uh-dar) in West Africa to the East Indies. In 1493 the Spanish government asked the pope to decide which lands Spain might claim. The pope "drew" an imaginary line running from north to south through the Atlantic Ocean. All new discoveries west of that line would belong to Spain. All new discoveries to the east would be Portugal's.

The pope's settlement was called the *line of demarcation.* Portugal soon protested the boundary, and talks were held between the Spanish and Portuguese governments. In 1494, the Treaty of Tordesillas (tord-uh-SEE-yus) came out of these talks. This treaty moved the line farther west (see map p. 169). Later, this second line allowed Portugal to claim Brazil.

But all the line-drawing did not stop the competition between Spanish and Portuguese explorers.

Around the Cape. In 1497 four ships slipped out of the port at Lisbon. They were commanded by Vasco da Gama (VAHS-coe dah GAH-mah), the son of a Portuguese nobleman. Like all Portuguese captains, Da Gama knew mathematics and navigation. He was a determined sailor, too.

Da Gama was attempting to make the greatest voyage Europe had yet seen. He was bound for India around the Cape of Good Hope at Africa's southern edge. The distances were immense. From the Cape Verde Islands to the Cape of Good Hope stretched 3,770 miles of open sea. And the Cape of Good Hope was only half way to Da Gama's destination!

In November 1497, Da Gama's fleet rounded the Cape of Good Hope. Nearly four months had gone by since the ships had left Lisbon. Now Da Gama began to make his way north along the east coast of Africa. He was sailing where no European had ever sailed before.

Progress was slow and painful. The ships had been battered by storms, and they were leaking. The sailors hadn't eaten fresh fruit and vegetables since leaving the Cape Verde Islands. As a result, many were sick with scurvy.

For a month Da Gama stayed on the shores of southeast Africa. He rested his men and repaired his ships. Then he pushed north again until he reached the coast of what is now Kenya. There Da Gama had a stroke of luck. He found a seafaring pilot who knew the route to India. In less than a month the pilot guided the fleet across the Arabian Sea. In May 1498, the fleet anchored in Calicut (KAL-ih-kut) on the southwest coast of India.

The voyage out from Portugal had taken nearly 10 months. The voyage home took 12. Four ships had sailed from Lisbon. Two returned. Half the sailors had died on the way.

For the Portuguese, the voyage was worth the cost. Vasco da Gama had found the sea route to the East. Their dream was now a reality. Da Gama's voyage helped make Portugal a world power. And, for the first time, it opened East Asia to Europe's other sea powers, including England and Spain.

Back in Lisbon, Da Gama told tales about his trip. Curious to find out more, King Manuel I of Portugal sent a second fleet to India. This one was much bigger than the first. The fleet was commanded by another nobleman's son, Pedro Cabral (PAY-droe kuh-BRAWL). He left for India in March 1500—and soon became involved in one of the most astonishing accidents in sailing history.

A Fortunate Mistake. It was impossible to sail from the Cape Verde Islands to the Cape of Good Hope in a straight line. In between lay the Gulf of Guinea (GHIN-ee), where the wind rarely blew. Sails would hang limp and useless for weeks. To avoid these calms, Cabral pointed his ships out to sea. He steered them southwest under a good wind. He hoped to pick up another wind far out in the ocean. This would hurry the ships southeast to the tip of Africa.

But Cabral sailed too far to the southwest. There he couldn't believe his eyes. Before him lay land. By accident he had stumbled across the South American coast.

M A P   E X E R C I S E

This map traces the routes taken by some of the explorers mentioned in this unit. Use the map to answer the following questions.

1. Who was the first of these European explorers to sail to the Cape of Good Hope?

2. Which navigator's voyage finally proved that the world was round?

3. From what two countries did most of the explorers begin their journeys?

4. Which of these explorers went the farthest north? What country did he sail from?

EXPLORATION ROUTES

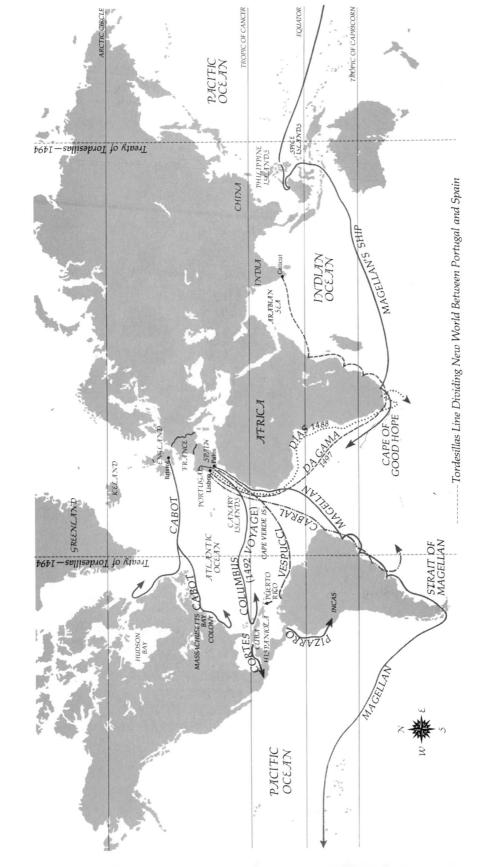

Tordesillas Line Dividing New World Between Portugal and Spain

DA GAMA   MAGELLAN

CABRAL

Cabral went on to India. But before he did, he sent word of his exciting discovery to King Manuel. Manuel sent sailors and ships to explore the new land. In time, it became a Portuguese colony—Brazil.

Da Gama and Cabral inspired other sailors who came after them. Of these, the most ambitious was a Portuguese captain, Ferdinand Magellan (muh-JELL-un). A few years after Cabral stumbled onto South America, Magellan headed in the same direction. His crew would not return to Europe until it had gone completely around the world.

Encircling the Globe. Like Da Gama and Cabral, Magellan was of noble birth. But for years he had served on Portuguese ships trading in the East. Now he felt entitled to a pay increase. Twice he approached King Manuel. Both times he was refused. Magellan left Portugal in anger and offered to serve King Charles I of Spain.

Magellan went to Charles with an inviting idea. He reminded the king of the

Treaty of Tordesillas. Then he put forth a plan of his own. Suppose, Magellan suggested, he found a way around the tip of South America. Suppose he then sailed west to the Spice Islands (now part of Indonesia). Wouldn't that prove the Spice Islands lay on the *Spanish* side of the line of demarcation? Wouldn't all the wealth and trade the islands offered fall to Spain?

Charles liked the idea. So, in September 1519, Magellan's fleet of five ships sailed from Spain. Thirteen months later Magellan reached the tip of South America. There he found a channel and entered it, hoping it wasn't a river mouth. Twenty days later he was at the other end. Magellan had proved there was a way around South America to the Sea of the South. He broke down and cried for joy.

The weather was fine, and the winds were fair. Magellan told his officers that they were "steering into waters where no ship has sailed before." Although Vasco de Balboa (VAHS-coe duh bal-BOH-uh) had crossed Panama to the Sea of the South six years before, he had not tried to sail a boat there.

Because the waters of the sea were so peaceful, Magellan named them the Pacific. The channel he had passed through later became known as the Strait of Magellan.

Now Magellan sailed on across the Pacific. As he went, he encountered a serious problem—lack of food. The drinking water was green with slime. The biscuit barrels were crawling with rats. One by one, the sailors died from scurvy. Some ate the ship's leather ropes. The lucky ones ate the rats.

Eighteen months after leaving Spain, Magellan reached the Philippine Islands. It was his last landfall. In the Philippines, Magellan sided with one group of natives against another. During heavy fighting, Magellan was wounded. Soon the local people killed him.

That left Juan de Elcano (wahn duh el-KAH-no), one of Magellan's officers, to complete the voyage. He limped home by way of Africa in September 1522. Five ships had sailed from Spain. Only one returned, leaking badly. The 17 men aboard it were described as "weaker than men have ever been before." They were also three years older.

Elcano received a reward from the Spanish king. It was a globe on his coat of arms. On it were the words: YOU WERE THE FIRST TO ENCIRCLE ME.

✎ Quick Check

1. *What was the* line of demarcation? *Why was it "drawn"? Why was a second line drawn?*

2. *What was the goal of Vasco da Gama's voyage? Who helped him reach his destination? How did the voyage add to Portugal's power?*

3. *How did Pablo Cabral discover Brazil?*

4. *Why did King Charles I support Magellan's voyage? What did the voyage prove? What problems did the sailors face? How did the voyage end?*

25
The Golden Kingdom

Exploration "fever" soon spread beyond Spain and Portugal. Other nations of Europe ignored the pope's line of demarcation. They sent their own voyages across the Atlantic. In 1497 and 1498, England sent an Italian seaman, John Cabot, to cruise along the Canadian and New England coasts. Cabot became the first explorer of the period to set foot on the North American continent.

By now Europeans were beginning to realize that the Americas were not Asia. Even so, explorers kept on sailing to North America under French, English, and Dutch flags. Many of them hoped to find a northwest passage to Asia through North America.

To the south, meanwhile, Spain was building its overseas colonies. It had established its first settlement on the island of Hispaniola, and it soon branched out from there. Spain sent out *conquistadores* (kun-KEY-stuh-doh-res), or conquerors, to win new territory. They were often joined by priests. The priests converted people who were living there to the Roman Catholic faith.

By 1530 the Spanish controlled the Caribbean. But the Caribbean was only part of the prize they sought. They were greatly interested in a story of a "Golden Kingdom" to the south. There, the story went, people drank from gold cups and ate from gold plates.

The story had special appeal to one Spaniard, Francisco Pizarro (fran-SEEZ-koe pee-ZAH-roe). Pizarro had had many adventures since arriving in the Caribbean in 1502. For a time he had been mayor of the town of Panama. He was known as a hard, silent man, and a good friend in a fight.

Pizarro hoped to be like his distant relative, Hernan Cortes (air-NAHN cor-TEZ). Cortes had sailed for Mexico with a small force in 1519. In two years Cortes had broken the power of the Aztec empire in Mexico. Cortes had made himself master of Mexico, and rich beyond anyone's dreams.

Greedy for Gold. Pizarro thought he could do the same thing in the Golden Kingdom—Peru. He went back to Europe to ask the permission of Spain's King Charles I. He returned with that permission and the titles of "governor" and "captain-general." The titles were supposed to give him control of 600 miles of the Pacific coast south of Panama.

Pizarro sailed from Panama in January 1530. He had a force of 200 men and some horses, rifles, and artillery. His four brothers and two partners were with him. One partner was a priest. The other, Diego de Almagro (dee-AY-go duh al-MAH-grow), was a soldier.

The country in which they landed was divided into three parts. It had a coastal desert to the west, a jungle to the east, and the massive Andes (AN-deez) Mountains in between. There, in the mountain valleys and plateaus, was the Golden Kingdom. It was the rich and powerful empire of the Incas. Ruling over that kingdom when Pizarro landed was Atahualpa (at-a-WALL-puh), the emperor. Like Pizarro, Atahualpa was a silent man who talked only when he had to. He seldom smiled.

Shortly after Pizarro's landing, Atahualpa began hearing of "bearded men with white skins." These strangers were said to carry sticks that spat death from a great distance. They rode animals that ran faster than the swiftest Inca warriors. The strangers seemed to prize gold and silver most of all. They were willing to fight and kill and die for it.

Atahualpa and his people thought of gold quite differently. To them, gold was a religious symbol. The Incas had lots of gold. They considered it useful but no more valuable than iron. They did not hoard it, and they certainly did not fight for it.

Atahualpa was curious to see these men who had come for gold. But he hesitated. Should he order his army to crush the "bearded whiteskins" and throw their bodies into the sea? Or should he meet with them?

Atahualpa's hesitation cost him more than he could have imagined.

The emperor finally agreed to a meeting with the white strangers. The meeting was to take place in the Inca town of Cajamarca (kah-huh-MAR-kuh). Pizarro needed a quick conquest. He knew his forces were no match for the Inca army. Treachery was his only hope.

Soldiers in the Square. Atahualpa and his men entered the main square of Cajamara. It was silent and empty. Atahualpa did not know that Spanish soldiers were hiding in the buildings facing the square. A priest stepped forward and handed Atahualpa a Bible. Then the priest asked the Inca emperor to accept

Christianity and the rule of Charles I. Atahualpa's answer was to throw the Bible to the ground.

At a signal from Pizarro, the soldiers began shooting. The soldiers were to kill as many Incas as they pleased. But they were not to hurt Atahualpa. The Incas were armed only with short wooden clubs. Most of them died in the hail of Spanish bullets.

Atahualpa was seized and thrown into a cell. There he remembered the Spanish love of gold. The Inca leader offered Pizarro enough gold and silver to fill his cell if he could go free. Pizarro accepted the offer and took the gold. But he backed out of his part of the bargain. He kept Atahualpa in jail.

Pizarro's partner Almagro believed that Atahualpa would always be a threat. Almagro persuaded Pizarro that the Inca king must die. Atahualpa agreed to be baptized as a Christian. Even so, he was sentenced to death by strangling, and that was how he died.

Now the Spanish marched on the royal Inca capital of Cuzco (KOO-sko). They took it without a struggle. In 1533 Pizarro became master of the Golden Kingdom. His dream had come true.

Francisco Pizarro lived violently. He died violently, too.

His partner Almagro was jealous of Pizarro's power. The two men quarreled over how to share the gold and silver they had taken from the Incas. Pizarro grew impatient with Almagro's increasing demands. In 1538 Pizarro gave orders

for his partner to be hanged as a traitor. The orders were carried out in Cuzco's main square.

But Almagro had a number of friends. They resented the execution and feared that they would be killed next. In 1541 they approached Pizarro's palace in the coastal city of Lima (LEE-muh). There they cornered Pizarro and took their revenge.

The Spanish in Peru continued to fight among themselves. Peace and order came only with the arrival of a new governor in 1569. Spanish rule continued until 1824 when Peru became an independent nation.

✎ Quick Check

1. *Where did Spain gain new territory? How did conquistadores and priests help in this effort?*

2. *What was the "Golden Kingdom"? How did the Spaniards find out about it? Give two reasons why Francisco Pizarro wanted to control it.*

3. *How did the Incas feel about their riches? About the "bearded whiteskins"?*

4. *How did the Spanish conquer the Incas? How did Pizarro die?*

EUROPEAN TRADE IN THE 1600's AND 1700's

This map traces trade routes taken by European and colonial traders over two centuries. Use the map to answer the following questions.

1. What area in Africa was a chief source of slaves?

2. What products were shipped from the Caribbean islands to the British colonies?

3. What products did the Europeans trade for slaves in Africa?

4. Name a principal port city in Portugal and one in England.

26
Human Bondage: European Slave Trade

In 1498 Christopher Columbus sailed to the Americas. His ships creaked under a new cargo—enslaved men and women from Africa. Columbus sold them to his former crewmates, the first Spanish settlers in Hispaniola. These settlers were building great farms, or *plantations*. They needed workers badly.

After Spanish explorers conquered the Incas, they tried to enslave them. The Spaniards needed workers to mine gold and silver and to grow crops. But the native Incas did not make good slaves. They had no resistance to European diseases such as smallpox. They died quickly from sickness, starvation, and overwork. Many killed themselves rather than submit to the Spaniards. So did many other groups of native Americans, such as the Mexican Aztecs and Mayas.

This left the Spanish settlers with plenty of natural resources but few workers. Soon they began to buy African slaves from European sea merchants. They hoped that Africans would be better and healthier workers. When this proved true, merchants began to import huge numbers of slaves to the New World. In the sixteenth century almost 900,000 slaves were imported. In the seventeenth century, 2,750,000 were imported.

At first only Spanish ships imported slaves. But soon French, British, Portuguese, and Dutch ships carried slaves as well. The Dutch soon dominated the trade. They carried 60 percent of all slaves across the Atlantic. Their slave traders worked for the Dutch West India Company, a powerful import firm.

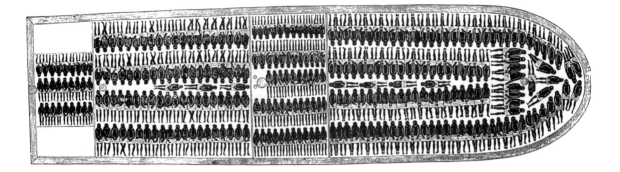

View of a ship's hold shows plan for transporting slaves to the Americas. Up to 35 per cent did not survive the journey.

People as Property. How did European merchants get slaves to sell? At first their sailors kidnapped people off the west coast of Africa. Slavery was nothing new to Africans. For centuries African chiefs had captured people in wars and used them or sold them as slaves. The Europeans soon found out they had things the chiefs wanted. Some tribal kings would trade slaves, gold, and ivory for cheap guns, iron bars, cloth, and rum. There were also African raiders who kidnapped slaves from their villages and sold them.

How could Africans be so cruel as to sell their own people? Perhaps it was because the life of a slave was bearable in Africa. Slaves in Africa had some rights. They could own property, marry, and inherit goods from their masters. If they worked hard, they could become rich and have slaves of their own. It is likely that most Africans had no idea how the people they traded would fare with European owners. Other African slave traders just didn't care.

When slaves were sold to European traders, they were first branded with hot irons. This identified the slaves as the property of the company that had bought them. Then the slaves were pushed into the hold, or lower part of a sailing ship. The holds were almost always hot, stuffy and filthy. Africans were chained together on rough wooden bunks. Each man usually lay squeezed in an area six feet long, one and one-half feet wide, and two and one-half feet high. One bucket was the toilet for everyone.

Of course, all ship captains wanted

their slaves to live until they could be sold in the Americas. So, for exercise, the slaves were forced to dance on deck. Some captains fed their slaves decent food and hosed them down regularly.

Despite these measures, many slaves did not survive the journey to the Americas. Deprived of fresh air for long periods and lying in filth, they died from diseases. Others killed themselves. Many of the Africans believed that their new masters meant to eat them at the end of the trip. To avoid this fate, some slaves jumped overboard if given the chance. They believed that when they died they would return to their native land.

Sometimes a ship's captain ordered slaves thrown overboard. This could happen when a slave rebelled or was too sick to be sold at a profit.

The Trade Cycle. If the ship arrived safely at a port in the Americas, the slaves were allowed to rest for a few days. Then they were sold at auction to the highest bidder. Healthy slaves between the ages of 15 and 35 brought the most money.

Most slaves were bought by Portuguese planters in Brazil and the Caribbean. There they were put to work growing sugar cane and making molasses and rum. Rum was traded for more slaves. This formed a vicious circle of trade. The more sugar, tobacco, and cotton a plantation produced, the more slaves it needed.

English settlers in North America used *indentured servants* for laborers. These

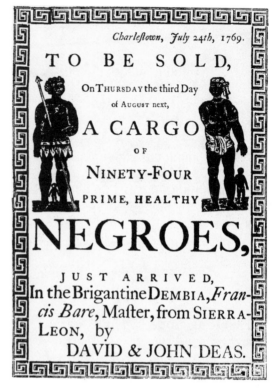

From 1451 to 1870, about 9.5 million slaves were shipped to the Americas.

people contracted to work for a master for seven years. In return, they received passage to the English colonies. However, plantation owners in colonies such as Virginia and South Carolina soon found that slave labor cost them less. So some cotton and tobacco planters there began to buy slaves.

Although some North American plantations had hundreds of slaves, their owners bought few slaves from Africa. Instead, they encouraged their slaves to have many children. Less than half a mil-

178

lion of the nine million slaves imported from Africa were sold in North America. The rest went to the Caribbean and Brazil.

A Slave's Life. When a slave was sold, he or she could usually expect a short life. Backbreaking labor in the fields, meager food, and regular beatings would probably be part of it. Slave uprisings were common, especially on the swampy Caribbean sugar plantations. Rebellious and runaway slaves were usually killed if caught.

Most masters viewed their slaves as machines who could work hard with little fuel or rest. Even those who were kinder to their slaves saw them as little better than work-animals. They cared for their slaves as they cared for their dogs or horses.

Also, most slaveowners did not respect the family ties of their slaves. Except in Brazilian slave markets, slave families could be separated when sold. Children were forever lost to their parents. Marriages were instantly ended.

A buyer inspects slaves at a Brazilian slave market. Most of the African slaves went to South America and the Caribbean.

Portuguese traders use native labor to power their ship.

Brazilian slaveowners did not separate families because they believed that slaves had souls. They converted their slaves to Christianity. They required them to attend church services. They also taught them to read and write.

On many plantations, a few slaves had some hope for a better life. Slaves who learned skills like cooking or horse-driving might become house servants or artisans. These slaves were usually valued and well cared for.

Voice of Protest. Most African chiefs supported the slave trade at first. But this changed when the chiefs realized they were losing their youngest, strongest, and most skilled people. Some chiefs tried to halt the slave trade. But the trade could not be stopped. Slave merchants could always kidnap Africans if they could not buy them.

One African king tried to protest this in 1526. He wrote to the king of Portugal, "Merchants who are allowed to come here . . . daily seize upon our subjects, sons of the land and sons of our noblemen and vassals and relatives . . . and cause them to be sold, and so great, Sir, is their corruption, that our country is being utterly depopulated." The Portuguese king did pay some attention to this letter. But the slave trade continued.

How did the slave trade affect Europe? It brought new wealth to Europe's rulers, merchants, and ports. Slavery was very profitable. A slave could be bought for a little rum and then sold in the Americas for hundreds of dollars.

European merchants grew rich by buying and selling slaves. This brought even more wealth to Europe. And Europeans could buy African gold and ivory, and American sugar, tobacco, and cotton at far cheaper prices than before.

European Views. But why didn't anyone protest against the shameful trade in human lives? Sixteenth- and seventeenth-century Europeans had different views of slavery than we have today.

Slavery had existed for a long time in Europe. Serfs only differed from slaves in that they could not be bought and sold. Also, people living on European coasts were in constant danger of being kidnapped by pirates. The pirates sold the Europeans as slaves in Muslim countries.

Even the Catholic Church had a long history of owning slaves. During the later Middle Ages, kings often made presents of slaves to the Church. One Christian abbey near Paris had 20,000 slaves. While the Church argued against enslaving Christians, it encouraged the enslavement of Muslims and other non-Christians. Christian masters felt they did their "heathen" slaves a great favor by converting them to their faith.

Nevertheless, some brave Europeans spoke out against slavery. In 1766 an English bishop named William Warburton preached against slavery. Warburton didn't agree that Africans were really better off enslaved than living in their native lands.

Some decades later, European thinkers wrote books and essays criticizing slavery. By this time, fewer slaves were being imported from Africa. Europeans no longer had as much to gain from slavery in the Americas.

Consequently, European nations began to pass laws that made slavery illegal. Great Britain was the first in 1807. By 1830, all European countries had outlawed the slave trade. However, slavery was legal in the Americas for another 50 years.

Some European merchants ignored the new laws. But the laws were an important step toward a new way of thinking in Europe. Some people recognized that they had no right to control the lives of others. They began to talk about new ideals like freedom and equality.

✎ Quick Check

1. *Why did Spanish settlers need slaves? Whom did they try to enslave? What happened to these slaves?*

2. *Give three ways that Europeans got slaves to sell. How were the slaves transported to the Americas? Describe the journey.*

3. *Describe the cycle of trade in Brazil and the Caribbean. What was life like for a slave? How did most masters view their slaves?*

4. *Why did African chiefs begin to protest the slave trade? Why didn't most Europeans protest against slavery?*

5. *Why did the use of slaves in Europe decline? When was it outlawed?*

PART 5
Review and Skills Exercises

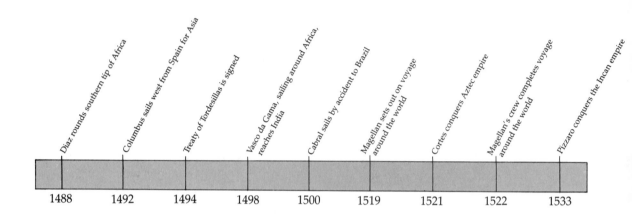

Diaz rounds southern tip of Africa

Columbus sails west from Spain for Asia

Treaty of Tordesillas is signed

Vasco da Gama, sailing around Africa, reaches India

Cabral sails by accident to Brazil

Magellan sets out on voyage around the world

Cortes conquers Aztec empire

Magellan's crew completes voyage around the world

Pizzaro conquers the Incan empire

| 1488 | 1492 | 1494 | 1498 | 1500 | 1519 | 1521 | 1522 | 1533 |

Understanding Events

Part 5 covers the period when some European nations were reaching out to other lands, making discoveries, and looking for wealth and trade. This period, called the Age of Discovery, brought drastic changes to the world. Study the time line and answer the questions.

1. Which occurred first, Diaz's trip to the tip of Southern Africa or Columbus's sailing for Asia?

2. When was the Treaty of Tordesillas signed? How many years ago was it signed?

3. What happened to Vasco da Gama in 1498? To Cabral in 1500?

4. When did Magellan's voyage around the world begin? Who completed the trip? When? How long did the journey take?

5. How many years before Pizzaro conquered the Incas did Cortes conquer the Aztecs?

Interpreting a Source

You have read that slave uprisings in the Caribbean region were common. Here is an excerpt about such uprisings adapted from *The Negro in the Making of America* by historian Benjamin Quarles. Read the excerpt and answer the questions.

The black codes [laws governing slaves] were most oppressive in cases of slave uprisings. . . . Of five slaves found guilty of conspiracy to revolt in Antigua, "three were burnt alive, and one hang'd, drawn, and quarter'd, and the other transported to the coast of central America." . . . Other means used to keep the Negroes from rebelling were the strengthening of the militia, the requirement that planters keep a specified percentage of white workers, and the deliberate mixing of Negroes of different tribal backgrounds. Since slavery was a means of control there was a strong reluctance to grant a bondman his freedom. . . . Despite all precautions, Negro uprisings became common in the West Indies. Slaves felt driven to revolt by the harsh treatment, and they were dared to take the step because of their large numbers. As early as 1522, a slave uprising in Hispaniola set the pattern for later outbreaks in other lands. . . . The French West Indies experienced the greatest of these outbreaks when, in the 1790's, Toussaint L'Ouverture led the slaves in Saint Dominique—later Haiti—to their freedom.

1. What were black codes?

2. How did white authorities try to prevent slave uprisings?

3. Why do you think white authorities did not want bondmen (slaves) to be given freedom?

4. According to the author, why were uprisings common in the West Indies?

5. Where was a slave revolt successful?

Building Vocabulary

Complete the following sentences by choosing the correct word or words from the list below to fill in the blanks. Write the numbers 1–7 on a sheet of paper. Write the answer next to each number.

1. _____ were sea warriors of Europe.

2. _____ were conquerors sent to other lands by Spain.

3. Sailors were helped in determining their position at sea by a _____.

4. Prince Henry of Portugal built an _____ to help train sailors in navigation.

5. Hernan Cortes conquered the _____ empire in _____.

6. Francisco Pizzaro captured the leader of the _____ empire and took _____ for Spain.

7. _____ could earn their freedom, but _____ could not.

slaves	conquistadores
Incan	compass
Aztec	indentured servants
Vikings	observatory
Peru	Mexico

PART
6
THE AGE OF
CHANGE

Anton van Leeuwenhoek (LAY-ven-hook) couldn't believe his eyes. He had just finished grinding a new glass lens for his microscope. Then he used it to look at a drop of rain water. He expected to see just a drop of clear water. Instead, he saw hundreds of tiny creatures swimming in that one drop.

It was 1677. Although microscopes had been around for 20 years, they were not very good. All the magnifying lenses had to be shaped and polished by hand. It took a lot of time and patience to make one good lens.

Leeuwenhoek was not even a scientist. He was a shopkeeper with very little education. His hobby was making lenses, which he used to look at things like plant seeds, wood, and sheep's wool. Now he sat and looked at the creatures in the water. Although he did not know it at the time, he had discovered a mysterious new world. It was the world of *microorganisms*, or living things too small to be seen with the naked eye.

Discoveries Close to Home. Leeuwenhoek was just one of many scientists who were discovering new worlds in the seventeenth and eighteenth centuries. One new world was the human body. William Harvey was a researcher who studied it. Using the *scientific method*, Harvey discovered how the blood circulates. First he got an idea, or *theory*, about how circulation works. Then he set up an *experiment*, or a way to test his idea. Finally he tested his theory about circulation many times. Because the tests supported his theory, he and other scientists accepted it as correct.

In the fifteenth and sixteenth centuries, explorers like Columbus and Da Gama had found new worlds in faraway places (see Chapters 23 and 24). Now scientists were the explorers. They made discoveries by observing everyday objects and events. Many of these discoveries changed the lives of Europeans. For example, Lazzaro Spallanzani (spahl-lahn-ZAHN-nee) discovered how to can food in 1765. This gave Europeans a new and wider choice of things to eat.   Some people thought that scientific discoveries were changing the world too quickly. These people were particularly bewildered by new ideas about the solar system proposed by astronomers (see Chapter 27). The English poet John Donne expressed the fears of the people of his time:

> And new Philosophy calls all in doubt,
> The Element of fire is quite put out;
> The Sun is lost, and th'earth, and no
>   man's wit
> Can well direct him where to look for it.

All-Powerful Rulers. Many Europeans living in the "age of change" looked to their governments for security. In some European countries, rulers had more power than ever before. They were called

Philosopher, René Descartes. Page 184: Louis XIV approves plans for a palace, glimpsed at top as a vision.

absolute monarchs, and they seized the right to make and break laws. They ruled with unquestioned authority and completely controlled their people. Louis XIV of France was one king who took absolute monarchy even further. He claimed he ruled by *divine right*, or by the will of God.

Some Europeans saw their absolute rulers as their parents. Catherine II of Russia was called Mother Russia, for instance. In times of trouble, absolute monarchs often rallied their subjects around them. For example, Elizabeth I of England spurred her sailors to battle a powerful fleet of Spanish ships. Rulers like Elizabeth helped encourage the spirit of *nationalism*, or loyalty to one's country.

They worked for their countries' interests and promoted its culture.

Thoughtful Criticism. At the same time, a few philosophers, or thinkers, began to question the idea of ruling by divine right. They formed a movement called the Enlightenment. They hoped to bring "light," or reason, to Europeans. Predictably, many Enlightenment philosophers were also scientists. They put their faith in reason as a means of discovering truth.

Enlightenment philosophers wanted the best for their fellow citizens. This did not mean that they openly promoted revolutions. Several philosophers even had close friendships with absolute monarchs. With the exception of Louis XIV of France, most rulers in Europe were interested in Enlightenment ideas.

Enlightenment philosophers wanted to improve existing circumstances. They did not want to cause radical change. Above all, they argued against injustice and unfairness. They believed in equality for all people, free speech, and representative government. They hoped for a world where scientific improvements would be matched by improvements in government and social justice. Their outlook was summed up by the seventeenth-century French mathematician René Descartes (reh-NAY day-CART): "Not only is progress possible, but there are no limits [to it that we can see]."

27
The Star Gazers

Scientists today know much of how the solar system works. But in the sixteenth century, most people did not know. Their ideas about the solar system came from an ancient Greek astronomer named Ptolemy (TAHL-uh-mee). He lived about 2,200 years ago. Ptolemy believed that the earth was the center of the universe. He said that the sun, stars, and planets traveled around the earth.

Ptolemy's ideas were generally accepted for more than 1,500 years after his death. As time went on, some members of the Catholic clergy began explaining them in religious terms. God had designed the universe with the earth in the middle, they said. They thought this showed the importance of humans to God. If the earth was the center of the universe, then it was easy enough to claim that humans played a principal role in God's design.

Early Observations. In the sixteenth century, a Polish man named Nicolaus Copernicus (koh-PURR-nick-us) also wondered about the universe. Like Ptolemy, Copernicus had a special interest in astronomy. From his youth, he had studied the movements of the stars. (He did so with his naked eyes, since the telescope had not yet been invented.) He had also been influenced by the writings of some ancient Greek philosophers. They had argued that the sun was the center of the universe.

Before long, Copernicus concluded that Ptolemy was wrong, and he began to say so. Some friends warned him against speaking out. To disagree with Church teachings could be dangerous. One who disagreed could be branded a heretic and possibly sentenced to death.

Copernicus, however, refused to back away from his own observations. He was

Copernicus (right) believed that the earth circles the sun.

a devout Roman Catholic and an official of the cathedral in his town. He had never denied that God had created the universe. All he was saying was that the earth was not at the center. He wanted to prove that Ptolemy was not correct.

Copernicus summed up his ideas in his book, *On the Revolutions of the Heavenly Bodies*. In it, he argued that the earth was a spinning ball in space. He tried to show by mathematics and logic that the earth and the planets travel around the sun. But in the sixteenth century that was not a commonly accepted idea.

He wrote the book in Latin over a period of many years. As he finished sections, he showed them to friends. When the book was complete, some of these friends had it printed in Germany. One of them made sure that Copernicus received a copy just before he died.

Copernicus's ideas were not widely accepted during his lifetime. Martin Luther, for example, thought Copernicus was a fool. It was years before most scholars paid serious attention to what Copernicus had said. By the end of the 1500's, however, some astronomers were examining Copernicus's ideas.

Around the same time, Catholic clergy began to notice Copernican theory. The theory disturbed them because it contradicted the Catholic idea of God's design of the universe. In 1616, more than 72 years after Copernicus's death, the Roman Catholic Church declared Copernican theory heresy. It also forbade Catholics to read his book.

Nevertheless, some scholars still studied Copernicus's ideas. One of them was a young German student named Johannes (yo-HAHN-ess) Kepler. He revised Copernicus's ideas to make them more precise. Copernicus, for example, had said that the earth traveled around the sun in a circle. However, Kepler felt that the earth moved around the sun in an oval path called an *ellipse*.

Proving Ptolemy Wrong. Another follower of Copernicus was an Italian, Galileo Galilei (gal-uh-LEE-oh gal-uh-LAY-ee). Galileo asked the question, "What causes the movement of the planets?" He was able to answer this with the help of a new invention. He ground some glass lenses and fit two together in a long tube. In this way, he made what he called a spy glass. It was the world's first telescope.

By looking through his telescope, Galileo made many new observations. He discovered that the Milky Way was made up of thousands of stars. As a result of his observations, he concluded that Copernicus had been right. The Earth *did* travel around the sun.

In 1632 Galileo published his own work on astronomy, the *Dialogue on the Two Great Systems of the World*. In it he tried to prove that Copernicus had been right. To do this, he described his discovery of four moons circling the planet Jupiter. This went against the idea that everything in the heavens rotated about the earth.

Galileo's *Dialogue* was published at a time when Pope Urban VIII was under great pressure. The pope reacted to the book as though it were a personal attack on him. Galileo was called to Rome to stand trial as a heretic.

In June 1633 he was found guilty of heresy and sentenced to prison. Galileo was forced to kneel and recant what he had said in the *Dialogue*. Then he was kept prisoner in his own house until his death.

The Catholic Church could ban books and deny ideas, but scientists continued to study the workings of the universe. Many of them accepted the beliefs of Copernicus and Galileo. But some wanted more proof. If the earth moved around the sun, what caused the movement? Why didn't the earth wander from its orbit and drift in space? What explained the fact that objects on earth fall to the ground? What explained the movement of the ocean tides?

All Things Must Fall. These and similar questions had bothered both Kepler and Galileo. Each had given partial answers to some of the questions. But neither had been able to end all doubt. That was achieved by an English mathematician named Isaac Newton. Newton proved to the satisfaction of most European scientists that Copernicus had been correct.

In 1687 Newton published a book, *Mathematical Principles of Natural Philosophy*. In it he explained the force that caused the earth's movement—the force we now know as *gravity*. According to Newton, every planet had its own gravitational force.

Newton called his idea the law of universal gravitation. The law applied not only to planets, but to every particle of matter in the universe. Newton's law helped explain the movement of the planets in their orbits. It explained why objects fall to the ground. It even explained the movement of the tides.

Newton's law of universal gravitation became the foundation for other scientific discoveries. It also began a period now called the Age of Reason. In this period, people started placing greater faith in human thoughts and ideas. In a sense, then, this law helped change Western thinking. Newton himself believed that he could not have succeeded without the work of earlier scientists. "If I have seen farther," he said, "it is by standing on the shoulders of giants."

✎ Quick Check

1. *What was Ptolemy's theory about the universe? What was Copernicus's theory? How was it different from the way the Catholic Church explained Ptolemy's ideas?*

2. *What did Galileo invent? What did he try to prove?*

3. *Why was Galileo called to Rome? What was the verdict? Why didn't the Catholic Church approve of Galileo's work?*

4. *What did Isaac Newton explain in his book? What did he call his idea? What new period did this law help introduce? How did people begin to change during this period?*

28
The Armada

In the 1580's, Spain's King Philip II had the greatest empire of any European monarch. He ruled Spain, Portugal, and the Netherlands. He governed many colonies overseas. His lands stretched from Mexico and Peru in the Americas to Goa (GO-uh) on the coast of India.

Philip's huge empire gave him great prestige. But just as ideas about the universe were changing, Philip's power and prestige would change too. A major force behind the change was a war on the high seas. This war has been called the first great international crisis in modern history.

King Philip feared war. He had already seen war at first hand, and been sickened by it. But Philip was angered by English seamen. For more than two decades, English sea captains had been robbing Spanish ships. One of these pirates,

Francis Drake, had sailed around the world, attacking and looting Spanish ships. When Philip demanded that the English give back the stolen goods, England's queen, Elizabeth, refused. Instead, she honored Drake by making him a knight.

Philip had other troubles with England. Philip thought of himself as a devout Roman Catholic. He was eager to help the Church win back some of the followers it had lost in the Reformation. Thus, he opposed Queen Elizabeth, a Protestant, on both religious and political grounds. For Elizabeth had begun helping Protestants in the Netherlands to free themselves from Spanish rule.

A Plan to Fight Back. Early in 1587, Philip decided to end the English threat. His plan was ambitious. He would put together the greatest fleet of ships the world had ever seen. The ships would head for England, carrying thousands of Spanish soldiers. They would gain control of the English Channel. Then a Spanish army waiting in the Netherlands could invade England. Elizabeth would be driven from the English throne. And there would be greater glory for the Spanish Empire.

The preparations went ahead all through the winter of 1588. Philip became quite impatient to get the invasion underway. By May 1588, his fleet, called the Armada, was ready to sail. There were 130 ships, carrying soldiers, horses, mules, and cannons. In all, the Armada held about 27,000 men. Not all of them were certain that they would conquer England.

The English, meanwhile, had heard about the coming attack. Some of Elizabeth's advisers had urged her to go into hiding to avoid capture. But Elizabeth refused and stayed with her people. As the time of the battle neared, she even visited the soldiers and tried to inspire them.

Later in the summer, Elizabeth summed up her own strengths. "I know I have the body of a weak and feeble woman, but I have the heart and stomach of a king," she said in one speech. The soldiers were stirred by such bravery. They realized their queen would stand by them. Elizabeth even won the admi-

ration of most English Catholics. They supported her, and England, against Catholic Spain.

A Surprise Victory. On July 30 the Spanish Armada began to sail up the English Channel. English sailors who saw the fleet were alarmed by the size of the ships. The English ships were much smaller and could not carry as many guns. It seemed that one shot from a Spanish cannon would be enough to blow an English ship to bits.

But when the fighting started the small English ships had an advantage. The English found that they could fire at a Spanish ship, then move quickly out of reach of its guns. Darting in and out, the English ships damaged the Spanish fleet. Even so, the Armada sailed along the entire south coast of England without suffering any major losses.

By August 6, the Spanish fleet had reached a point near Calais (kah-LAY), France. The next night the English struck. First they tried to set the Armada on fire. Next the English attacked and badly damaged the Spanish ships. Then a storm came up to cause further damage. By August 12, it was clear that the Armada had been defeated.

Only about half of the Spanish ships escaped sinking or capture. They tried to return to Spain by sailing completely around England. On their way home, some of them were wrecked in the

Queen Elizabeth I (right) appears triumphant over the Spanish Armada (background) with her right hand on the globe.

194

Mary Stuart, "Queen of Scots" (above right), and Philip II of Spain (above left) were the main threats to the power of England's Queen Elizabeth I.

stormy northern seas. Disease broke out among the sailors and soldiers. By the time the Armada limped into Spanish ports, the Spanish had lost thousands of men. The English had lost about 100.

Quarrels Continue. The English sailors came home to a huge celebration. Victory fires lit up the sky over London. King Philip's plan to conquer England had been stopped. The English would continue to be a power on the high seas.

But the defeat of the Armada did not settle the dispute between Spain and England. The two countries remained at war until 1603. Nor did the fighting in the English Channel put an end to Spanish sea power. Spain was stung by its losses. It rebuilt its navy and became more powerful on the seas than ever before.

Yet, the Armada's defeat did deliver a major blow to Spain's prestige. Before the battle, the Spanish had moved from triumph to triumph. No other European power had been able to stop them. But after 1588, the rest of Europe knew that Spain could be beaten. Spain would remain Europe's most powerful nation for many more years. But the period of its greatest glory had now passed.

✎ Quick Check

1. *Why was King Philip having troubles with England? What was Philip's plan to stop the English threat?*

2. *How did Queen Elizabeth show her loyalty to her people? What religious groups supported her? Why?*

3. *Describe the battle in the English Channel. Why did England win? After the defeat of Spain, how did the world's view of Spain change?*

29
The Sun King

He was called the Sun King and the Grand Monarch. He lived in a palace with enough rooms to house 10,000 people. Everything in it was either made of gold, covered with gold, painted gold, or embroidered with gold.

Gold was the color of the sun, and the sun was the symbol of France's most powerful king, Louis XIV. The palace, called Versailles (ver-SY), took 47 years to build. It may have cost as much as $100 million. But Louis would spare no expense. "Let it be done to accord with our greatness," he told the architects.

Versailles was a fitting home for a king who claimed that he was chosen by God to rule France. Louis was thought to be responsible to God alone for his actions. It was believed that God had given Louis the right to rule. This was called *divine right*.

When his grandson became king of Spain in 1700, Louis told him, "You must be master. Never have a favorite nor a prime minister. Consult your council [of ministers] and listen to what they have to say, but decide for yourself. God, who has made you a king, will give you the necessary wisdom. . . ."

In the seventeenth and eighteenth centuries, many European monarchs claimed they ruled by divine right. But none played the role better than Louis XIV. One writer called him "the greatest actor of royalty the world has ever seen." Even as a boy, he impressed everyone with his kingly manner.

The Sun King was born September 5, 1638, to Queen Anne and King Louis XIII of France. From his mother Louis got both a strong Catholic faith and a belief in *autocracy* (government by one ruler).

She told him that resisting a king's will was a sin against God, as well as against the king.

From the time he was a child, Louis always seemed to know what to say. When it appeared, in May 1643, that his father was dying, Louis was asked, "Do you want to reign?" Louis, who was not yet five, replied with tears in his eyes, "No, I do not want my good Papa to die." Yet Louis XIII was anything but a "good Papa." He was, in fact, a cruel, suspicious man who made his family miserable.

Four days after his father's death, Louis made his first official appearance as king. Of course, Louis was much too young to rule France. Cardinal Jules Mazarin, acting as prime minister, had the real power.

Young Louis disliked books. He preferred fencing and dancing lessons to studying. But he listened carefully when Jules Mazarin began to teach him about politics. Distrust everybody, especially ministers, Mazarin said, for they will try to deceive you. Don't let any other member of the royal family become powerful. Keep your business secret. Be stern with those who ask for favors. Take the people's money, but spare their lives.

When Mazarin died in March 1661, Louis showed how well he had learned his lessons. He immediately announced he would rule France without a prime minister. He would control the government personally. "I am the state," he declared.

The young king was extremely ambitious. He wanted his reign to be glorious. There were two paths that led to glory, Louis believed. One was to build great palaces. The other was to increase his country's territory by military conquests. Louis decided to try both.

Life at Versailles. The palace of Versailles was located about 10 miles from Paris. It was meant to dazzle and impress everyone. Priceless paintings by the world's greatest artists hung on the walls

Jules Mazarin, prime minister, diplomat, and Louis XIV's political teacher

Vast and splendid, Versailles cost many millions and took 47 years to complete. Louis XIV moved the court and government from Paris even before the first stage of building was finished.

of the Throne Room. Other walls were paneled with mirrors that reflected huge crystal chandeliers.

Yet it would have been hard for visitors not to notice that the palace also had some drawbacks. The chimneys smoked too much. There was too little heat. In severe winter weather, bottles of wine froze.

The most striking problem was the tiny size of the rooms housing the members of the nobility. But the nobles could

hardly complain. They stayed at Versailles at King Louis' expense. In reality, of course, the French taxpayers paid for their upkeep. More than half of all the money collected in taxes was used to maintain the court.

How did the nobility spend their time at Versailles? One noble woman described a typical day in a letter to a friend. From early in the morning to three o'clock in the afternoon she hunted. Then she went to her apartment and changed into full court dress. Afterward she gambled until seven. From the card tables she went to the theater to see a play. That was followed by supper at 10:30. Finally she went to a dance that lasted until three o'clock in the morning.

Both Louis and his queen, Marie Thérèse (teh-REHZ), participated in these activities. For example, they both gambled heavily. In fact, the queen often lost thousands of dollars before noon. The queen also spent much of her time with her dogs. The dogs shared her meals and had their own servants.

At Versailles, the nobles had little to do but serve and amuse the Grand Monarch. They also flattered and imitated him. When Louis began to wear a wig to hide his baldness, all the nobles shaved their heads and wore wigs. When he had indigestion after dinner, they made the same complaint. They listened breathlessly to his remarks, no matter how unimportant. If the king looked on any one of them, that man or woman was the envy of all.

So much flattery was bound to affect Louis. As time went on, he became more and more proud and boastful. Yet he also had good qualities. He was a kindly man who could be generous even toward his enemies. Once, for example, a court priest named Francois Fénelon (fran-SWAH fain-ul-OWN) wrote a pamphlet attacking Louis. Fénelon criticized the Sun King's great wealth. He pointed out that many French people were poor and starving. He even called Louis' devotion to his religion "superficial."

Did Louis put the outspoken clergyman in prison? Not at all. He promoted him to the rank of archbishop in one of the richest cathedral towns in France.

Too Much Spending. Court life was luxurious, but Versailles was draining France's wealth. So too were the almost constant wars that Louis fought. During his long reign, France became involved in four expensive conflicts that spanned almost 50 years. Louis saw himself as a great warrior-king and military planner. He was indeed a brave man who often stood in the line of fire to show his courage. But he often embarrassed his generals, who had to find easy targets for Louis during combat. Like his ministers, his generals flattered him.

Louis' attacks on neighboring states made some of Europe's most powerful rulers unite against him. In 1702, England, the Netherlands, the Holy Roman Empire and others allied against France. They wanted to keep Louis' grandson off the throne of Spain. From then on, the French army suffered a series of disastrous defeats.

The picture at right shows Louis XIV, a shrewd statesman, signing a treaty with Switzerland. During his reign, France became the diplomatic center of Europe.

Soon the costs of the war brought France close to *bankruptcy*, or financial collapse. Raising taxes did not help because the people had no more money. Louis had to beg for loans to keep his government going. He even tried to sell his jewels, without success.

Then, in 1709, an unusually cold winter and spring brought even more suffering to France. The number of deaths from cold and starvation in the area of Paris alone was estimated at 24,000. Yet the government had no money to buy and import grain for bread. The once-great army had no food, arms, or uniforms. It was ready to quit.

The People React. Revolution was threatening the French government. That August a mob of hungry Parisians marched on Versailles. From his window, the king could hear the crowd shouting in the streets. People made bold speeches against the government and Louis. The king could do nothing to halt them.

At the last moment, Louis and France were saved by a change of government in England. Exhausted by the war, England was as eager as Louis for peace. So the new English government signed a secret truce with France. England dropped out of the conflict. When a general peace treaty ended the war in 1713, France escaped complete defeat. But France was now poor and in debt. It had been reduced to the rank of a second-rate power.

Louis lived to be almost 77. His reign of 72 years was the longest in European history. In his lifetime he made France the center of western European life. He also made many enemies along the way. But even his enemies admired his accomplishments. When he died, someone said, "When I heard of the death of Louis XIV . . . it had the same effect upon me as if I had heard of a splendid old oak [tree] . . . laid flat upon the ground by a storm. He had stood upright for so long."

But there were more people who resented Louis XIV for his abuses and excesses. Long after Louis died, the French would remember how his lavish lifestyle and needless wars harmed their country. They would remember the absolute power of the Sun King when evaluating later French rulers. These harsh memories would lead to a new movement among the French to replace the monarchy with a republic.

✎ **Quick Check**

1. *What was rule by divine right?*

2. *What was Mazarin's advice to Louis? What two paths to glory did Louis want to follow?*

3. *Describe the palace of Versailles. Who lived there? Who paid for its upkeep? Describe a typical day at the palace.*

4. *How did Louis XIV drain Franace? How did Parisians react to the problems Louis caused? Why? What change did bad memories of Louis bring about?*

30
The
Enlightenment

In the eighteenth century, Paris was a major center of culture. Writers, thinkers, and artists met in *salons*. A salon was a gathering of people in a private home to discuss ideas. Educated women held these social events. The meetings were meant to encourage art and music, and the exchange of new ideas. The wittiest and most talented artists, musicians, and writers were invited.

Salons were also held to promote the development of new art forms. For example, a musician might compose a new kind of music. Salon members would help make it popular.

The Four Philosophers. There were four people who were especially favored guests at salons. They were Voltaire (vohl-TAIR), Jean-Jacques Rousseau (zhahn-zhahk roo-SOH), Denis Diderot (duh-NEE DEE-droh), and Baron de Montesquieu (du mahnt-uhs-KYOO). They were the most important *philosophers* of eighteenth-century France. Philosophers are people who study ideas in order to reach an overall understanding of life.

These four men came from different backgrounds and often disagreed with each other. However, they shared some major ideas. They all believed in *reason* — the ability of humans to think and make decisions by using facts. They all believed that there was an order to the workings of nature, and that people should follow that order. And they were all dedicated to the ideals of progress, freedom, and equality.

Many women who ran the salons admired these philosophers. But one

An evening at Madame Geoffrin's Paris salon. An actor reads beneath a bust of Voltaire. His audience includes Denis Diderot and Jean-Jacques Rousseau.

woman was more successful than any other in getting them to come to her salon. She was wealthy, cultured Thérèse Geoffrin (teh-REHZ zhaw-FRAN). She held her salon every Monday and Wednesday. On Monday she met with painters, and on Wednesday, philosophers. She also exchanged letters with the brightest people of her era. She was always surrounded, Diderot said, "by all that are of any importance, whether in the capital or in Court."

If Madame Geoffrin had kept a diary of her salon and her opinions of it, what would she have written?

August 6, 1757

My salon was a great success today. Madame Chandon (shan-DOH) played a charming new song by that German composer, Joseph Haydn (HIDE-en). I have written to Haydn and invited him to come and play it here himself.

Diderot and Rousseau were also here today. Diderot is very upset because the seventh volume of his Encyclopedia has been banned. I think this is ridiculous. The Encyclopedia is a brilliant work. It tells about many great scientific discoveries. It has many good articles on politics. Also, it has all sorts of articles on practical subjects, such as cheesemaking.

Rousseau and Diderot do not seem to be getting along lately. Today they argued about the place of women in society. Rousseau believes that women should stay at home. He says they should be educated only on how to run a house and raise children. Diderot thinks that women should be free to learn about the world.

I agree with Diderot. Women are proving their ability to learn things that used to be only for men. They are even becoming scientists! Voltaire's great love, Émilie du Châtelet (AY-mill-ee do sha-teh-LAY), is a brilliant scientist. Besides, I don't think Rousseau has the right to put down women. After all, it was a woman, Madame Warens (WAHR-ahn), who helped support him and his family for years.

Even though I was a little angry at Rousseau, I forgave him when he started talking about his new book. It is called The Social Contract. It will start with the phrase, "Man is born free, and everywhere he is in chains." This means that our society makes us into slaves. Rousseau says that the book will be about his ideas on improving society. He believes that in the ideal society, each person is both the ruler and the subject. By this he means that everyone must help make the laws, and that each individual is equally important.

Not everybody at the salon agreed with Rousseau. Some said that the common people cannot be trusted to make laws. But Rousseau says that the people must be educated. He believes that the ability to think and reason comes from a good education.

Denis Diderot was in debt by the time he finished his Encyclopedia.

Frederick the Great (standing), an important patron of the arts, deep in discussion with the writer Voltaire.

January 10, 1758

I just received a long letter from Voltaire. He has written a new book that will surely stir up a lot of discussion. It is called **Candide**. *Voltaire told me that he wrote it in three days! Actually, I'm not surprised. Despite his poor health, he never stops writing plays, essays, and delightful letters.*

Voltaire kindly enclosed a copy of the book, which I finished reading last night. It is about a young man named Candide who starts out believing that we are living in "the best of all possible worlds." After Candide suffers greatly, he comes to see that this is not true. He realizes that the world can be cruel and unjust. Finally, he decides that the best thing to do is to face up to things as they really are. He chooses to use reason, not superstition, as a rule to live by.

Voltaire can be so daring. Unfortunately, that quality has gotten him jailed and kicked out of France more than once. He has always criticized those who don't let people of different religions worship freely. Yet he makes fun of religious rituals and superstitions. He even says that people should not hope for miracles. Some clergy have gotten mad at him for that. Unfortunately, they don't realize that Voltaire has always had great faith in God. Above all, he believes that people should behave morally in all things.

I hope that my good friend Voltaire will be able to return from Switzerland soon. We miss him here in Paris, and at my salon!

March 10, 1761

Today our king, Louis XV, announced that he will take all responsibility for ruling France. This reminded me of the ideas of my late friend Baron de Montesquieu. I hunted up the Baron's book, The Spirit of Laws, *and reread it.*

The Baron would never have approved of the way Louis rules. The Baron always said that government should be divided into three parts. First, the king or queen should have executive power. This means that he or she would appoint public officials, head the army, deal with other countries, and see that the laws are carried out.

According to the Baron, the second branch of government should be legislative. This branch would have the power to make laws. Montesquieu believes that this part of the government should be made up of talented nobles.

The Baron says that the third part of government should be some kind of high court. Lawsuits could be settled there.

The whole point of Montesquieu's three-part government is that no part has too much power. Also, each part can use its power to limit the powers of the others. That way, no person or group of people can have complete authority over everyone else.

Montesquieu's system has worked in England. I wonder if it can succeed in France?

Many of the ideas discussed in Madame Geoffrin's salon were not widely known elsewhere. Fortunately, she invited many foreigners to her salon. They went home to their own countries with new books and new thoughts. Madame Geoffrin helped to spread Enlightenment thought to all parts of Europe and to North America.

✎ Quick Check

1. *What were the* salons? *Who gathered there? Why? Who ran the most successful salon?*

2. *What three ideas did Voltaire, Rousseau, Diderot, and Montesquieu share?*

3. *Describe the contents of Diderot's* Encyclopedia. *What was the argument between Diderot and Rousseau? Describe the point of view of each side.*

4. *What is the title of Rousseau's book? What does Rousseau's phrase, "Man is born free, and everywhere he is in chains" mean?*

5. *What is the title of Voltaire's book? What does the main character discover about the world? How does he deal with it?*

6. *Describe Montesquieu's three-part system of government. What is the main benefit of it?*

31
The Woman Who Brought Europe to Russia

In 1744 an awkward teenaged girl named Sophia arrived in Moscow after a long, cold journey. She was immediately introduced to Elizabeth, empress of Russia. Elizabeth wanted her nephew, Peter, to marry Sophia. Peter was the heir to the title of czar. Although nobody could predict it then, Sophia was to become one of Russia's greatest rulers. She would bring important changes to Russia.

Sophia Augusta Fredericka was the daughter of the prince of a small, poor, German state. Sophia was only 14 when she reached Moscow. But she was ambitious and mature for her age. Peter, on the other hand, was an immature, bad-tempered boy of 15. Despite his faults, Sophia agreed to marry him. She knew that the wife of the czar of Russia could have great wealth and power.

Surprisingly, Sophia and Peter became friends. However, just before their marriage, Peter caught smallpox. He survived the deadly disease, but it left him permanently scarred. Sophia could not hide her dismay. Still, Empress Elizabeth insisted they get married.

Sophia changed her name to Catherine, which was thought to sound more Russian. Then she married Peter. Catherine spent her time studying Russian language and culture. She loved to read, and tried to educate herself as much as possible. She admired the philosophers of western Europe, especially Voltaire, Montesquieu, and Diderot.

Although Peter was to become czar, he did not try to learn Russian. In fact, he hated everything about Russia. He spoke longingly of his home in Germany. He

Catherine the Great took over the throne from her husband Czar Peter III.

Catherine Is Crowned. Catherine didn't get along with Peter or his mother. Then, when Catherine was 31, Empress Elizabeth died. Peter became Czar Peter III. Unfortunately, he acted as if his new title gave him the right to do as he pleased. He made the Russian army angry by signing a peace treaty with Frederick the Great. He further insulted his soldiers by ordering them to go to war against the Austrians, their former allies. He also angered the powerful Russian Orthodox Church by threatening to seize its property. Ordinary Russians thought he was crazy.

In the meantime, Catherine won the hearts of the people. She tried to behave like a patriotic Russian. Whenever Peter humiliated her in public, the people took her side.

Six months after Peter became czar, Catherine arranged to have him arrested. One of Catherine's advisers murdered Peter in prison. Shortly afterward, Catherine was crowned empress.

Catherine set out to rule as an all-powerful but thoughtful leader. Although she had absolute power, she hoped to use it to benefit her people. She wanted to govern according to the theories of the Enlightenment philosophers.

Unfortunately, the ideas of the Enlightenment were difficult to apply in Russia. These ideas often seemed reasonable, but failed when put into practice. Catherine once said to Denis Diderot, "You work only upon paper, which endures all things . . . but I, poor empress as I am,

openly admired Frederick II, also called Frederick the Great, who was the king of Prussia. This made Peter look bad because Russia was at war with Prussia. In short, Peter did many things that made Russians dislike him.

Russian pride grew under Peter the Great, especially among peasant serfs.

work on the human skin, which is irritable and ticklish to a different degree."

Philosophy vs. Real Life. Catherine had a major problem. Should she change the system of serfdom in Russia? Enlightenment philosophers were completely against any kind of forced labor.

Nine out of 10 Russians were serfs. They suffered far more than serfs in western Europe. They could be bought and sold like slaves. They could be forced to work seven days a week. If they farmed, they were not allowed to keep their crops. But not all of them were farmers and laborers. There were serfs who were artists, too. Like serfs who worked the land, they were often abused by members of the upper class. For example, any noble could own a troop of actors, dancers, or musicians—and beat them for a displeasing performance.

Catherine did not care for serfdom. But unlike the philosphers, she believed that serfs were made serfs by nature, not by human law. She also knew that the great landowners would rebel if the serfs were freed. As a result, Catherine did not try to outlaw serfdom.

Catherine explained her decision to maintain serfdom in an essay. She wrote,

"To make such a sweeping change as the freeing of the serfs would not be the way to make oneself loved by the landowners." Rather, she tried to improve serfs' lives. She wanted to improve the chances that a baby born to serfs would survive. She wanted to stop the nobles from torturing their serfs. She even hoped to curb the practice of putting people to death as punishment.

Unfortunately, most of Catherine's planned changes never happened. And others made little difference, at best. In fact, Catherine created more serfs by enslaving three million free Ukrainians. The life of every serf became worse.

How did this happen? In 1773 a soldier named Emelyan Pugachev (poo-guh-CHAWF) led a huge serf uprising. Pugachev posed as Peter III, who, he claimed, had not actually died in prison. Pugachev roamed the Russian countryside promising freedom to the serfs. He encouraged them to revolt against their masters. Pugachev was eventually caught and executed.

Catherine tallied the deaths and property damage the rebellion caused. She did not feel sorry for the serfs, whom she had originally set out to help. Instead, she sympathized with their masters. She made punishment for rebellion stiffer. And she gave all nobles absolute power over their serfs. Thus, she actually made life worse for most of her people.

Enlightened Achievements. Catherine was more successful at applying other new ideas. For instance, she gave more religious freedom to Roman Catholics and Jews. Her greatest achievement was bringing the culture and learning of western Europe to the Russian people.

Fifty years earlier Russia had been almost untouched by Western ideas. Then Czar Peter I, also called Peter the Great, visited the great capitals of western Europe. He decided to make many changes

Peter the Great studied Western methods in Holland in order to modernize Russia.

in Russia based on what he had seen in western Europe. For example, he had Russian men cut off their beards because European men were clean-shaven.

But Peter's reforms went much farther. He increased Russia's trade with the West. During his reign, Russia produced new goods in new factories. In addition, Peter encouraged the arts and started the first Russian newspaper.

Catherine continued along the path of progress begun by Peter the Great. Trade with Europe tripled during her reign. Russian nobles began to wear European clothes and copy European manners.

The empress also encouraged the development of writing, art, and music. Fifty years after Catherine's death, Russia had some of the finest writers in Europe. Catherine also built free schools where many Russians learned to read. She built hospitals and the first Russian medical school.

Catherine died in 1796 after a reign of 38 years. Was her reign a success? Under her rule, Russian culture reached new heights. Russia became a wealthier nation and it entered the modern age.

Unfortunately, human rights came to mean almost nothing in Catherine's Russia. But things would change. By bringing the ideas of the Enlightenment to Russia, Catherine paved the way for further progress. Russians would begin to see serfdom as unfair and unneccessary. Finally, 65 years after Catherine's death, her great-grandson Alexander II would free the serfs.

Peter the Great cuts off a gentleman's beard, a symbol of traditional life.

✎ Quick Check

1. *What was Peter's attitude toward Russia? What was Sophia's attitude?*

2. *Give two reasons why the Russian people turned against Peter after he became czar. How did Catherine become ruler of Russia? How did she want to govern Russia?*

3. *Describe what life was like for serfs in Russia. Why didn't Catherine free the serfs? In what ways did she hope to improve the lives of serfs? Why and how did she make their lives worse?*

4. *Give two ways that Catherine brought Enlightenment ideas to Russia.*

RUSSIA MOVES TOWARD EUROPE

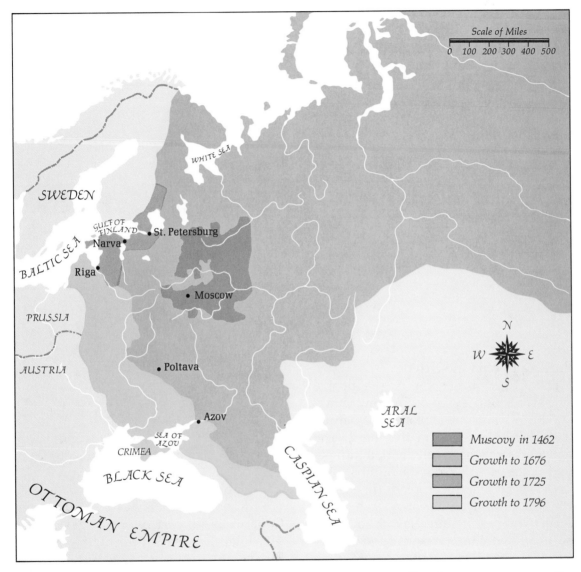

This map shows the expansion of Russia from 1462 to 1796. Use the map to answer the following questions.

1. In which period was Russia's territorial growth the greatest?

2. The Baltic Sea is a route that connects Russia to many European ports. In what period did Russia first gain access to this trade route?

3. Locate the Crimea. During what period was it gained by Russia?

4. What is the distance between Riga and Azov?

PART 6
Review and Skills Exercises

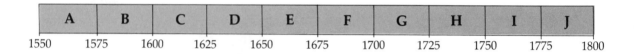

A	B	C	D	E	F	G	H	I	J

1550   1575   1600   1625   1650   1675   1700   1725   1750   1775   1800

Putting Events in Order

Part 6 described some of the people and events of the Age of Reason. Thinkers during this time explored the natural world and the world of the mind. The time line above has been divided into periods lettered A–J. Write the numbers 1–9 on a sheet of paper. Read the list of events below. Decide when each event occurred. By each number write the letter of the period when the event took place. You may use some letters more than once. Refer to your text to help you.

1. Galileo publishes book on astronomy.

2. Isaac Newton publishes book on theory of gravity.

3. The English defeat the Spanish Armada.

4. Anton van Leeuwenhoek discovers microorganisms.

5. Louis XIV begins to rule France.

6. Spallanzani discovers how to can food.

7. Catherine the Great of Russia dies.

8. Roman Catholic Church declares Copernicus's theory of universe heresy.

9. Pugachev leads uprising of serfs in Russia.

Interpreting a Reading

During the Enlightenment, men had most of the opportunities to do scientific research. Still, many women devoted themselves to science and made valuable

214

contributions. One of these women was Maria Sibylla Merian. Merian was born in Germany in 1647 and died in Holland in 1717. Read the article about her and answer the questions.

She Studied the Smaller Creatures

In 1699 Maria Sibylla Merian set off for South America. Her aim was to study the insects and plants in the Dutch colony of Surinam. Such a trip was unusual for a woman of the time. Travel was then uncomfortable and could be dangerous. It was not unusual for Merian, who had traveled around her native Germany studying insects. Her interest in entomology, the study of insects, had taken her to other places in Europe, too. When one of her daughters married a Dutch merchant in Surinam, she decided to travel there to study insects in their own surroundings.

Merian had created a new way to learn about insects. Instead of working with dead specimens, she collected eggs and caterpillars and raised them. As she watched the insects changing, she drew accurate and beautiful pictures. She showed each insect in its life stages with the kind of food it liked. Merian was a gifted artist. This talent helped her produce a catalog of flowers and another of European moths, butterflies, and other insects.

Merian was 52 years old when she went to Surinam. She spent two years there observing, recording information, and making pictures. In 1705 she published a book on the insects of Surinam. The book added to the knowledge of plants of South America. Merian included many carefully drawn pictures of trees and fruits. Later, science honored Merian by giving her name to some newly discovered plants.

1. What is the name for the study of insects?

2. What was new about the way Merian studied insects?

3. Besides a keen interest in insects, what talent did Merian have that helped her with her research?

4. Why do you think Merian was so interested in the plants that the insects lived on?

Understanding Terms

Each sentence below contains an underlined word or term that appears in Part 6. Read each sentence carefully and decide if the underlined word is used correctly. Write the numbers 1–5 on a sheet of paper. If the word is used correctly, put a checkmark next to its number. If the word is not used correctly, write a sentence using the word in a correct way.

1. Microorganisms are part of the solar system that must be viewed through a telescope.

2. Ruling by divine right meant that a king received the power to rule from God.

3. The Enlightenment was a movement to spread European culture to Africa.

4. The Age of Reason produced many thinkers, or philosophers, in Europe.

5. A French salon of the eighteenth century was an elegant meal for royalty.

PART
7

AN AGE OF REVOLUTION

What causes a revolution? One answer can be found by looking at one of the most revolutionary periods in all of history. Between 1641 and 1795, France, England, and England's American colonies all had violent revolutions. People in all three nations revolted against absolute monarchs.

Behind all revolutions there are common causes. Governments which start out serving the people may become inflexible over time. People begin to see their world differently. What seems reasonable and right in one age is later seen as harsh and unnecessary. Governments are often too slow in adjusting to new ideas.

A century before their revolutions, the French and English people, as well as the American colonists, were satisfied with absolute monarchy. Few complained, for example, when Elizabeth I ruled England with an iron hand. Why? Because people thought her rule was good for them and for England. She strengthened England's navy and kept the country safe from invaders such as the Spanish. England was peaceful and prosperous. People had a strong sense of belonging to their country. Patriotism meant loyalty to the queen.

People Demand Rights. The monarchs who fell to revolutions all made similar mistakes. One involved religion. In England, for example, King Charles I tried to impose his Anglican religious beliefs on the Presbyterian Scots. This con-

tributed to unrest among both the Scots and the non-Anglican English.

Another big mistake the monarchs made was to tax people either too much or unfairly. French peasants resented paying heavy taxes while nobles neither worked nor paid taxes. The English did not want to pay taxes to wage wars or maintain the king's court. American colonists refused to pay taxes to support the English army. They disliked paying taxes to which they hadn't agreed.

The English and the French revolutions were similar in other ways. In the first stage, revolutionaries swept away old customs and privileges but kept the monarch on the throne. The second stage was more violent. Revolutionaries killed the monarch and turned power over to the people. In the third stage, the radicals lost their power, but some changes brought by the revolution were kept. Throughout all three periods, patriotism came to mean loyalty to the cause of revolution, rather than to the old system.

Certain new phrases from these revolutions became familiar slogans. Words such as *liberty* and *equality* were the slogans of the times. These slogans owed a debt to the philosophers of the Enlightenment. During the revolutions, these words took on special passion. They reflected the idea that people deserved to be treated with more respect by their governments. And they expressed a belief that things could be changed for the better.

In 1776, Patriots pulled down the statue of George III in New York, symbolically overthrowing their master, England.

32
The English Revolution

Ever since the Middle Ages, kings and queens had ruled England with the help of Parliament (see Chapter 9). But over the centuries, English rulers often struggled with parliaments for power. In the 1600's, one such struggle became a revolution against the absolute monarchy.

From the time he became king in 1625, Charles I had little contact with ordinary people. He preferred to stay at his court. He did not trust Parliament, and Parliament did not trust him. They could not agree on anything.

One reason for the disagreement was religious. Many leaders of Parliament belonged to a Protestant minority group, the Puritans. They were also called Roundheads because the men had short hair which showed the shape of their heads. Puritans followed the teachings of John Calvin (see Chapter 19). Mainly, they sought to *purify*, or cleanse, the Church of England. They thought that the clergy should not wear robes and that rituals should be more simple. Charles sided with those who valued ritual. He was against Puritanism and fought it.

Taxing the Poor. Charles's problems with Parliament were not only religious. For example, he thought Parliament had the duty to let him set taxes. The people of England groaned to think of paying more taxes. Although their taxes were among the lowest in Europe, most people were poorer than they had ever been. The cost of goods had almost doubled since the death of Queen Elizabeth in 1603. But most people's pay had hardly increased at all.

Nevertheless, Charles imposed many new taxes to help pay for several unsuccessful wars. Parliament began to question the rights of their king. One member of Parliament wrote, "All our liberties [are ruined] if the King might at his pleasure lay what unlimited taxes he pleased upon his subjects, and then imprison them when they refused to pay."

In 1629 Charles needed money for a war with Spain. When Parliament refused to let him collect more taxes, he dismissed Parliament and collected the taxes anyway. He forbade Parliament to meet again for the next 11 years.

Without Parliament, Charles felt freer to go his own way. He and his supporters kept on trying to drive the Puritans from the English Church. Then, in 1634, Charles declared that England faced a national emergency and set a special tax. This angered many people and raised new questions about the king's authority.

Thirteen years later, the revolution began. Charles fled London. He formed an army of supporters, called Royalists, and prepared to fight against the Puritans.

The English Revolution was a *civil war* in that English fought English. Friends and families split up on opposite sides of the conflict. It was a *revolution* in that it brought a change in the type of government.

Finally, Charles's army was defeated. He was brought to trial. To put a king on trial was an extraordinary show of power for the law. People must have been amazed and even frightened. Here is how they might have talked about this incredible event.

The time: January 20, 1649

The place: outside Westminster Hall, where King Charles I is on trial.

The action: Trevor De Gwynn, a Royalist, and Michael Corby, a Puritan, are arguing. De Gwynn is a poet from a noble family. Corby is a wealthy merchant. They are old childhood friends who are split by their different beliefs.

DE GWYNN: I never thought that the people of this nation would sink so low. To put their own king on trial!

CORBY: It had to be done. Charles has ignored the wishes of the people for years. Do you remember when he declared a national emergency in 1634? He used that as an excuse to tax us further! He acted as if Parliament didn't exist. He only let Parliament meet when he wanted more money. And if they disagreed with him, he refused to let them meet.

DE GWYNN: He had a right to do so. The king doesn't answer to Parliament. He has only to answer to God.

CORBY: I can't believe that God approves of how Charles spends his tax money. He wastes money on troops for unnecessary wars. And he spends a fortune on his court and entertainment. Do you know how much his last *masque* (a short play) cost? Two hundred pounds! That's more than I earn in two years. While laborers can hardly buy bread, the king watches stiff actors wearing velvet and feathered masks.

DE GWYNN: *I* was invited to that masque.

I thought it was brilliant. Should the king give up all art and beauty for want of money?

CORBY: I'm not suggesting that. But very few people benefit from the king's court entertainments. Besides, acting is sinful. I've been trying to convince you of that for years.

DE GWYNN: Oh, you Puritans don't know how to enjoy yourselves.

CORBY: How can we enjoy ourselves when we are not even allowed to worship God in our own way? When the king appointed Archbishop Laud to head the Church of England, we had no peace. Laud threw people in prison if he suspected them of worshiping like Puritans. Sometimes he even had their ears cut off! It was a great day when we got rid of Laud. But Puritans are still not safe.

DE GWYNN: How can you complain of violence when your leader, Oliver Cromwell, is the most violent of all? I don't trust Cromwell an inch. He only wants to rule England himself.

CORBY: Cromwell will save this country, you will see. He is a great general. Eight years ago, no one would have believed that the Royal Army could be beaten. But Cromwell beat it with a bunch of farmers!

DE GWYNN: Look, people are coming out of the courtroom. Let's find out what happened.

(De Gwynn and Corby approach a man who is leaving the courtroom.)

CORBY: Sir, would you tell us about the outcome of the trial? We were forced to wait outside.

MAN: I wish I had done the same. It was one of the saddest things I have ever seen. The king sat like a stone while they accused him. He was too proud to defend himself. He said that his accusers had no legal right to put him on trial. Finally, they sentenced him to death. You know, I've been against King Charles from the start. But the very thought of killing our own king makes my blood run cold.

DE GWYNN: They will not dare! Something will surely save him.

Despite the hopes of some Royalists, the sentence was carried out. To the end, King Charles refused to defend himself, saying that he was only to be judged by God. He was beheaded six days after the trial. England became a republic.

England's first and only written constitution, the Instrument of Government, was prepared. In 1653 Oliver Cromwell was named Lord Protector. His rule was limited by this constitution and by Parliament. But members of Parliament kept quarreling with each other and with him. To maintain order, Cromwell ignored Parliament just as King Charles had.

Imagine that De Gwynn and Corby meet again two years after Cromwell comes to power.

DE GWYNN: Well, Corby! I haven't seen you since the king's trial. How have

After Charles I's execution (above), England became a republic. Oliver Cromwell (lower right) was named Lord Protector in 1653.

been very difficult too. Last year, he decided to go fight in Cromwell's army. First they trained him. Then he was shipped off to fight some Irish rebels. The rebels were fighting against the English rule of Ireland. It turned out, though, that Cromwell did not only want to kill the rebels. He sent Geoffrey and the other men into the town of Donegha and ordered them to kill *everyone*, even the Catholic priests. Nine thousand Irish were killed on that one day. Cromwell was very proud of that battle and thanked God for it. But Geoffrey was disgusted. He ran away from the army and came home.

you and your family been?

CORBY: We are all in good health, thank God. But I'm worried about my son Ben. You wouldn't know him. He's 16 now. Well, he's been in a lot of trouble with the law lately. He was put in jail for organizing a cockfight (a kind of sporting event played with roosters). Then, when he got out, he was fined 20 pounds for swearing! He said something which I won't repeat about our Lord Protector.

DE GWYNN: I suppose you don't care for Cromwell as much as you did, eh?

CORBY: Well, I don't want my son swearing or doing other sinful things. But I do think that my wife and I should be the ones to punish him, instead of the government.

DE GWYNN: My oldest son Geoffrey has

CORBY: I heard about that battle too. But I was too busy worrying about paying my taxes to worry about the Irish. You know, Cromwell taxes us as heavily as King Charles did. He dismisses Parliament when they disagree with him. Sometimes I think we've exchanged one bad ruler for another.

After Cromwell died in 1658, England fell into confusion. The people decided to return to monarchy. Charles I's son came to the throne as Charles II. He was careful to consult with Parliament about most of his decisions.

The next king, James I, was a Roman Catholic. He took the throne in 1685. As a Catholic he was a threat to Protestant control of the government.

Cromwell dismissing the Parliament, soon after he gained power

Thus, another conflict seemed to be brewing. This time England's ruling classes were determined to avoid civil war. In 1688 Parliament invited James's daughter, Mary, and her husband, William of Orange, to become joint monarchs. James found he had no supporters left and fled England.

This changeover is known as the Glorious Revolution. In making it, Parliament took no chances. Before crowning William and Mary, Parliament had them sign an agreement. Known as the Bill of Rights, it spelled out the basic powers of Parliament. Like the Magna Charta, the Bill of Rights is considered a victory for the rule of law.

✎ Quick Check

1. *What was King Charles I's attitude toward ordinary people? Toward Parliament? Toward the Puritans?*

2. *Why did Charles tax the English people? What conflicts did the taxes cause? What eventually happened to Charles?*

3. *Why was the war in England a civil war? Why was it a revolution? Who was fighting whom?*

4. *Who was Oliver Cromwell? What was supposed to limit his power? Why didn't it work? In what ways did Cromwell turn out to be like King Charles?*

5. *What was the Glorious Revolution? How did it come about? What did the Bill of Rights say?*

33
Conflict in the Colonies

The Enlightenment philosopher Voltaire once said, "Everything that's happening today is spreading the seeds of a revolution." He was right. A decade after his death, revolution ripped through his own country, France. But the first major revolution of the late eighteenth century did not take place in Europe. It occurred in Britain's 13 colonies. They stretched along the Atlantic coast of North America from New Hampshire to Georgia.

The American colonists had long been an independent people by nature. Many of them were Puritans who had left England to escape the harsh rule of King Charles I. In America they had been joined by other people searching for change, from Scotland, Germany, and elsewhere. Over several decades, the hard life of the unsettled frontier made these people more independent.

For most of the eighteenth century, Britain had ruled the 13 colonies with a light hand. The colonies enjoyed more self-rule than any colonial people anywhere. Then, in 1763, Britain won a war against France and got control of much more of North America.

The war had been expensive. Many British leaders believed that the colonists had not paid their share. After all, the war had been waged to defend the colonies. Even after the war ended, the British still had to keep their troops in America. This was to protect colonists from local Indian raids. Many British leaders were determined that the Americans should pay some of this expense.

Unpopular Acts. In 1765 Parliament passed two laws with this idea in mind. One required Americans to provide housing, transportation, and supplies for

On March 5, 1770, British troops fired on a crowd in Boston, killing five colonists. The "Boston Massacre," depicted in this engraving by Paul Revere, helped sow the seeds of revolution.

British troops. The other said that newspapers and other printed material used in the colonies had to carry stamps. This was called the Stamp Act. The money Americans paid to buy the stamps would be used to support British troops.

Americans soon insisted on their rights as English subjects. They complained that they were being taxed without any voice in the matter. "Taxation without representation is tyranny," was the colonial cry. This reaction so alarmed British leaders that they backed down. In 1766 Parliament *repealed,* or canceled, the Stamp Act.

Seven years later another act of Parliament caused further trouble. In 1773 Parliament allowed a British company, the East India Company, to sell tea to local merchants in the colonies directly. This meant that colonists could buy tea more cheaply than before. But it also meant that American traders who had been bringing tea into the colonies were excluded. The colonists objected, setting the stage for full revolt.

Late in 1773, three English ships loaded with tea arrived in America. In Boston, colonists boarded the ships and dumped the cargo overboard. Many

In this cartoon, the colonists have tarred and feathered the British tax collector.

Americans thought this was going too far, but they agreed with the idea behind it. The tea was refused at nearly all American ports.

King George III and his government reacted angrily. The way they saw it, they had treated the American colonies gently. They believed they had a right to collect taxes from the Americans. But they had given in to the Americans—on everything except the tea issue. And that disagreement alone did not justify disobeying the laws.

Tougher Measures. The British government decided to crack down. It introduced several bills in Parliament. One would close the port of Boston to all trade. Another would tighten control over the local government of Massachusetts.

There was heated debate in Parliament. Several members opposed the bills. But the government insisted on tough measures. The prime minister, Lord North, asked, "Will you sit still while the colony attacks your subjects and breaks your laws?" The bills against Boston and Massachusetts were passed by a large majority.

Meanwhile, a group of Bostonians had gotten together. They offered to pay for the destroyed tea. But when they heard the news from Britain, they withdrew their offer.

The news of the two bills touched off anger throughout the 13 colonies. The Virginia legislature passed a vote of sympathy with Massachusetts. The royal governor quickly dissolved the legislature, but its members met again at a nearby inn. They sent letters to other colonies, proposing that representatives of all 13 meet to discuss their problems.

The Massachusetts House of Representatives had the same idea. All over the colonies, most Americans wanted to work together. The British government had pushed them too far. Early in September 1774, 56 representatives met in Philadelphia. Among them were George Washington from Virginia and John Adams from Massachusetts. They started the first Continental Congress.

Neither Side Retreats. In October 1774, the Congress agreed on a Declaration of Rights. It declared that Americans had liberties based on "the laws of nature." It demanded that Britain end many of its controls in the colonies. And it backed these demands by saying that the colonies would refuse to buy any British goods.

The Declaration arrived in London just before Christmas. It was discussed in Parliament after the holidays. Again the debate was heated. Some leading members, such as the famed speaker Edmund Burke, defended the Americans. They said that many of the Americans' demands could and should be met. Outside Parliament, many English people brought petitions asking for a peaceful settlement.

The British government did not want war. "I do not wish to come to severer measures," said George III. But, he added, "We must not retreat. The colonies must either give way or defeat us."

A majority in Parliament agreed. Brit-

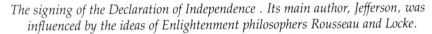

The signing of the Declaration of Independence . Its main author, Jefferson, was influenced by the ideas of Enlightenment philosophers Rousseau and Locke.

ain would not retreat, and the colonies would not give way. What would happen now? A member of Parliament gave his view: "In a few years, independent Americans may celebrate a glorious revolution of 1775, as we do that of 1688."

War Breaks Out. The first shots of the war did come in 1775. In August 1776, another declaration from the Continental Congress reached London. "When in the course of human events . . . ," it began. "All men are created equal . . . ," it continued. And it ended by saying that "these United Colonies are, and of right ought to be, Free and Independent States."

The Declaration of Independence was a turning point in American history. It meant that the colonists could not back down. In 1778 the Americans won a major victory at Saratoga, New York. France now joined the fighting against its old enemy, Britain, but the war still dragged on.

Then, in October of 1781, the British were trapped at Yorktown, Virginia. The British general, Lord Cornwallis, surrendered. Finally, on September 3, 1783, the British signed the Treaty of Paris. It recognized the 13 colonies as a new republic, the United States of America.

American leaders next set out to form a government strong enough to hold the 13 states together. In May 1787, a Constitutional Convention met in Philadelphia. Following the example set in the English Revolution, it drew up a written constitution. This Constitution called for a fed-eral system in which the states would yield some powers to the central government. It also called for a system in which one branch of government would limit the powers of another. This idea had come from the Baron de Montesquieu (see Chapter 30). It became known as a system of *checks and balances.*

In some ways, the Americans had followed the same pattern as the English Revolution. They had insisted that governments get their power from the people they govern. The French watched while some of their people fought for this idea in America. Now they began to want it for themselves.

✎ Quick Check

1. *What two laws did the British Parliament pass in 1765? Why? How did the American colonists react?*

2. *What events led some colonists to dump tea into Boston Harbor? How did Parliament respond to this action?*

3. *What was the Continental Congress? Where was it held? What did the representatives declare? What did they demand?*

4. *Why did war between England and the colonies break out? How did the Declaration of Independence affect the war? How did the war end?*

5. *What was the purpose of the Constitutional Convention? Name two principles of government called for by the Constitution. Why was the system of* checks and balances *so important?*

34
Storm over France

France in 1789 was like a keg of dynamite waiting to go off. The nation of 24 million people was the largest, wealthiest country in Europe, but its government was broke.

How was this possible? France simply spent more money than it collected in taxes. The problem was not that the country spent too much. It raised too little in taxes. The nobles and the clergy, the largest property-holders in France, paid few taxes.

The nobility still had great power. Many of the customs of feudalism that dated from the Middle Ages were still in place (see Chapter 5). This meant that the nobles had special privileges. They collected money from peasant farmers on their feudal manors, but passed little along to the government.

These feudal practices were not only draining the government, they were hurting the poor people of France. Spe-

cial privileges for the lords meant that it was hard for poor people to better themselves. It meant that food prices were high and pay was low.

Impossible Odds. King Louis XVI was faced with a crisis in 1789. It was not his fault. He had taken over a government on the verge of bankruptcy. The kings before him had spent money recklessly on wars. They also gave the nobility more privileges.

Louis has been unfairly considered a mean-spirited tyrant. On the contrary, most historians agree that he was a fair-minded king. He tried to find ways to end the crisis facing his country. Louis' main fault was that he couldn't make decisions. This is a serious failing for a leader. His wife, Queen Marie Antoinette (mah-REE an-twah-NET), added to his difficulties. She loved fine things and had little sympathy for the poor. Marie-Antoinette was so disliked that most peo-

Marie Antoinette, as painted by a contemporary, Elizabeth Vigée-Lebrun.

ple believed an ugly rumor about her. It was said that she heard that the poor were crying for bread. "Let them eat cake," she supposedly replied.

In 1789 Louis was forced to call a meeting of a special assembly called the Estates-General. The Estates-General was made up of three groups, or estates. The First Estate was the clergy. The Second Estate was the nobility. The Third Estate was the common people.

The king had hoped that the Estates-General would vote for more taxes. This would put a quick end to the crisis.

The nobility did not want to give up their privileges. And neither they nor the commoners wanted to pay more taxes without getting something in return. Both groups wanted more political power. Before this struggle was resolved, neither France nor the European world would be the same again.

The trouble began before the meeting of the Estates-General. The assembly had not met since 1614. Louis had asked a court in Paris to tell him how the group should meet. The court, controlled by the nobles, ruled that the group should meet according to its old rules. This meant that each estate met and voted separately. This way, the votes by the first two estates together would be able to outnumber the third.

The Voice of Dissent. The lawyers and businessmen of the Third Estate refused to accept the old rules. There were new ideas of liberty and equality in the land. Members of the Third Estate argued that they were the most important people in France. The nobility, they argued, was an old-fashioned idea from the Middle Ages.

When the Estates-General met at the royal palace at Versailles outside Paris, the members of the Third Estate refused to meet as a separate group. They left their meeting place. At an indoor tennis court on the palace grounds they declared themselves the National Assembly of France. The members also swore the *Oath of the Tennis Court,* promising to write a constitution for France. The revolution had begun.

All eyes now turned to King Louis

XVI. Members of the National Assembly were still hopeful that the king would go along with them. The nobles and clergy reminded Louis that the National Assembly was talking as if it, not he, was the rightful ruler of France. Louis hesitated. Then he sided with the nobles. Louis called 18,000 soldiers to Versailles.

In Paris the news of the National Assembly came on top of bad economic news. Many working people were out of work. Others were on strike. Riots broke out about working conditions and the price of bread.

Independence Day. People were nervous about the soldiers in Versailles. Groups of people began to arm themselves. On July 14, one group set off for the Bastille, a fortress and prison in Paris. At the Bastille, the crowd demanded the governor give them his cannons and other guns. In the confusion a battle broke out. The enraged crowd surged into the Bastille and killed the governor, soldiers, and other officials. The seven prisoners in the fort were freed.

The storming of the Bastille was the opening of the bloody battle that was the French Revolution. To those fighting for change, it was an inspiring moment. To this day, French people regard July 14, called Bastille Day, as Americans do July 4.

By the summer of 1789, the National Assembly was controlling the government of France. In the beginning of August it ended feudalism. This did away with all the special privileges of the no-bles and the debts that peasants owed them.

Later in August the National Assembly passed the *Declaration of the Rights of Man.* This document was a statement of the principles of the revolution. The assembly declared that all people had the rights of freedom and equality. The words of the Declaration: "liberty, equality, fraternity (brotherhood)," became the battle cry of the revolution.

Turmoil in France. The events of the summer pushed the revolution forward. But all of France was not in favor of what was happening. Nobles hated losing their privileges. They thought it shameful when a group of angry peasant women dragged the king to Paris. To them, the common rabble had insulted the dignity of the king.

French people were turning against each other over the revolution. Many important nobles left France. They went to other countries in Europe. There they pleaded with fellow aristocrats to help the nobles of France. The leader of the nobles was the Count of Artois (are-TWAH), the king's brother.

Inside France, people were divided over a new law of the National Assembly. It took away all property belonging to the Catholic Church. The new law went further. It made all priests employees of the government. This new law bitterly divided the French. Religious Catholics turned against the revolution. Fighting broke out in the provinces against the revolutionary government.

In 1791, King Louis XVI secretly left Paris. He tried to flee the country to join his brother and other nobles. His carriage was stopped near the German border, and the king was returned to Paris. The assembly and its supporters now considered the king a traitor to France.

King Louis XVI was tried and convicted of *treason,* or attempting to overthrow the government. A slim majority of the assembly voted that Louis should be put to death. The next day, the king courageously faced the *guillotine* (GIL-uh-teen)—a device used to kill people by cutting off their heads. He was beheaded in front of a large crowd.

The kings of Europe had already begun to make war against France. The supporters of the French Revolution were ready. They were fighting for a cause, their newly won liberty. French armies not only met the invading armies. They threw them back and invaded neighboring countries. In each country, the French spread the ideas of liberty, equality, and fraternity.

A priest says the last rites to Louis XVI on the platform of the guillotine.

✎ Quick Check

1. *Why did the French government raise so little money in taxes? How did feudal practices hurt the poor?*

2. *Why was France on the verge of bankruptcy in 1789? What was Louis XVI's main fault as a ruler?*

3. *What three groups made up the Estates-General? What did Louis XVI hope this meeting would accomplish? What did he ask the court to decide before the meeting? What did the court rule?*

4. *What did the members of the Third Estate refuse to do? What action did they take? What happened at the Bastille on July 14?*

5. *What did the* Declaration of the Rights of Man *proclaim? Why did the nobles oppose the revolution? Why did religious Catholics turn against the revolution? What happened to the king? Why?*

35
The Terror

The new leaders of the French Revolution began to give up the idea of a monarchy completely. Many of these leaders belonged to a Parisian political club called the Jacobins (JAK-uh-bins). They wanted a whole new way of life. They wanted to put into practice the ideals of the Declaration of Rights.

The leaders made plans to spread their ideas throughout Europe. The leaders of other European countries were horrified. Soon France was at war with Austria, Prussia, Britain, and the Netherlands. In France itself, rebellion burst out in different parts of the country. Nine months after King Louis was executed, his wife Marie-Antoinette was put to death. Government leaders were determined to punish all who spoke against them.

Georges Danton (DAHN-tawn) was one of the most popular leaders of the revolution. He was energetic, bold, and an outspoken defender of the rights of the people. When foreign armies began threatening France, Danton rallied the French. He inspired them to defend their country.

Fighting for What? But in time even Danton believed that the revolution was going too far. He had a rival, Maximilien Robespierre (ROBES-pee-air). And Robespierre was calling for stronger action still. Like Machiavelli, Robespierre was convinced that to get control, any action was justifiable. He wanted to get rid of anyone who disagreed with the revolutionary government. This meant using the guillotine.

Crowds carrying wax busts of unpopular public figures gathered in Paris streets to hear speakers call for change.

For 12 months, Robespierre decided who was an enemy of the country. Anyone he accused was usually beheaded. Hundreds died each week, in what came to be known as the Reign of Terror. After a while, no one was safe—not even leaders of the revolutionary government.

Let's look at what happened to one revolutionary.

"Georges Jacques Danton, you are accused of treason against the people of France!"

The date was the seventh of Germinal in the Year 2. This was April 3, 1794. The revolutionaries had invented their own calendar. They wanted to make a complete break with the past.

It was an unusually hot day for April. The Paris courthouse was jammed with spectators. Danton, a tall, powerful man, stood in the prisoner's dock. "Me, a traitor?" he roared. "Citizens, you all know me. I've always worked for the people, never against them."

Nicolas Herman, the president of the court, rang his bell. Robespierre had warned Herman not to let Danton begin a speech. They had hoped to shut him up by putting him in a group trial. He was in prison along with several friends and some criminals. But Danton was a hard man to silence.

"Do you expect me to keep quiet when people are telling lies about me? What kind of men dare call me a traitor?"

Some of the crowd started applauding. Herman rang his bell. "Danton!" he shouted. "You won't get anywhere by trying to accuse the jury."

"I'm not accusing anyone. I'm defending myself! I've devoted my life to this country. I helped to make the republic. I helped organize an army to fight our foreign enemies. I created the Committee of Public Safety to rout our enemies here at home. And then I tried to hold it back when it went too far. Yes, citizens, it went too far! The republic was safe. The foreign enemies were driven back. But the committee went on sending hundreds, thousands of people to the guillotine. It wasn't just nobles, priests, and rebels who were killed. People were being hunted down for other reasons. Because they were suspected. Because they were disliked. Because they were people like me — Danton!"

The crowd cheered. The prosecutor

Marat exclaims to Robespierre (seated) and Danton on the horrors of the revolution.

passed a note to Herman. The prosecutor passed a note back. Both men looked uneasy. Robespierre had warned them that Danton must be found guilty—or *they* would go on trial. Herman quickly declared the court closed for the day.

During the next two days of the trial, Danton was not given a chance to speak. He was told that he could give a final speech of defense. But when the time came, he was hustled out of the dock. He stopped to roar for the last time: "You are murderers!"

Then he called on someone who had carefully stayed away from the trial. "Robespierre!" His voice could be heard far out in the streets. "You too will go to the guillotine! You will follow me, Robespierre!"

Danton Dies. After Danton left, the jury found him guilty and sentenced him to death. That same afternoon, three wagons rolled away from the jail. They headed for the public square where the guillotine was set up. Danton sat in one of the wagons with his friends. He tried to cheer them up.

At the scaffold, Danton had a long wait. The sun was setting as he walked to the guillotine. For a moment he stopped, suddenly afraid. Then he said: "Come on, Danton—no weakness!" and turned to the executioner. "Show my head to the crowd afterward. It's worth the trouble."

He lay down. The executioner fastened his neck in the slot. The blade came swishing down.

Now Robespierre was master of the revolution—but not for long. He pushed the Reign of Terror so far that no one was safe. A tavern keeper was killed for selling bad wine. Priests died simply because they were priests.

By July 1794, the other leaders of the revolution turned against Robespierre. Robespierre tried to shoot himself. He was carried, bloody and screaming, to the guillotine. The Terror was over.

About 30,000 French people had been executed in the past year. Only one sixth of them were nobles. Now the French reacted against the ideas that started the Terror. They took to heart the words of Madame Roland, who died in the Terror. "Oh liberty," she cried, "what crimes are committed in your name!" The people were tired of violence. They were ready for any moderate government that could give them peace and quiet.

✎ Quick Check

1. *What did the Jacobins want to do? Who was Danton? Who was Robespierre? How was Robespierre like Machiavelli?*

2. *Why did the revolutionaries create their own calendar? Give two reasons why Danton believed the revolution went too far.*

3. *What did Danton predict for Robespierre? What did Danton ask his executioners to do?*

4. *Who turned against Robespierre? Why? How did Robespierre's death affect the Reign of Terror? What was the mood of the French people following the Reign of Terror?*

36
Man of War

The French Revolution and the wars that followed created great opportunities in France for ambitious people. At the start of the nineteenth century, a young soldier named Napoleon Bonaparte took advantage of this. Napoleon came from the the island of Corsica, south of France. All his life, he believed he was meant to do great deeds. As a young soldier he did not just follow orders. He made a scientific study of every battle he was in. Soon the young officer felt he knew more than his commanders.

Napoleon was very good at planning and organizing battles. Before long, government leaders in Paris noticed him. In 1799, Napoleon was appointed to head the government during a period of unrest. As leader of France, Napoleon began a series of wars. France won most of the wars and gained new lands.

Napoleon also restored order in France. He broke the power of the radical supporters of the revolution. But he also brought many of the ideas of the revolution into the French government.

By 1804, Napoleon had crowned himself emperor of France. He was on his way to spreading his empire all across Europe. Then four European countries joined forces to stop him. They succeeded. In 1815 his armies were defeated for the last time at Waterloo.

Napoleon was sent to St. Helena, a small island in the South Atlantic. He was warned never to return. There, he died in 1821. This is how three Frenchmen might have discussed the news of Napoleon's death.

JEAN-PIERRE: What sad news! The emperor is dead.

ALFONSE: Sad? I'm not sure. He did a lot

Napoleon crowns himself emperor with the 1000-year-old crown of Charlemagne.

for France. But he was also ambitious and vain. That's what finished him off, you know. He just kept scheming to get more. It made you wonder whether he cared more for France or himself.

HENRI: Napoleon care for France? Ridiculous! He deserted his men several times on the battlefield. He only came back to Paris because there was political advantage to be gained. This man made his brothers, sisters, and all his other relatives rulers of the countries he conquered. Napoleon a patriot? You must be kidding!

JEAN-PIERRE: Now wait just a minute here! I served with the emperor. He was a leader, a military genius. How else can you account for the great victories we won? I remember the Battle of Jena in 1805. Those Prussian troops looked so sure of themselves. But we ran them right off the field. Look at the record: Belgium, Holland, Prussia, Austria, Italy, Poland. We conquered almost all of Europe.

ALFONSE: I sympathize with you, Jean-Pierre. You must find this news of Napoleon's death sad. I always envied your stories of those great victories. But you are leaving out the stories of the terrible losses. First there was the naval disaster at Trafalgar off the coast of Spain in 1805. Remember how Admiral Nelson of the British Navy destroyed the French fleet? Without the fleet, Napoleon had to drop his plans for invading England.

HENRI: Yes, and there was also the disaster in Spain. Napoleon conquered the country. But the Spanish took to the hills and never stopped fighting. Spain cost us many soldiers.

JEAN-PIERRE: You are right. I do leave those out. And it is still hard for me to talk about the disaster in Russia. I remember proudly marching off to Russia in 1812. We were the largest army in the world. There were 700,000 of us. With the emperor leading us, we believed we could not be beaten. Certainly, no rag-tag Russian army was going to defeat us. And they didn't. It was the weather that got us.

ALFONSE: Tell Henri about it, Jean-Pierre. He's never heard you tell this story.

JEAN-PIERRE (shudders): It makes me cold just to think about it. The Russians knew they couldn't beat us. So they kept retreating. And when they retreated, they burned the fields and killed the livestock. So, soon we were far from our bases and couldn't live off the land. We did not fight a real battle until Borodino, outside Moscow. We beat them, of course, but we lost a lot of men. When we entered Moscow, we couldn't believe it. The Russians had burned the city, so there was no shelter or food. Then we started to go back. And winter came. It snowed and snowed. The wind howled. Oh, it was terrible. Men were dropping everywhere. We ate horses and mules. And then we ate nothing. You know that great army of 700,000 men I mentioned

Napoleon's army attacks the Russian city of Smolensk, in 1812.

earlier? More than half a million never made it home.

ALFONSE: Yes, that was the beginning of the end. The Prussians beat Napoleon at the Battle of Leipzig in 1813. In 1814, Napoleon gave up the throne. A council of all the leaders of Europe met at Vienna. They agreed that Napoleon should be sent to Elba, the island off the coast of Italy. They also insisted that Louis XVIII, Louis XVI's brother, be made king.

ALFONSE: Yes, that was too much for Napoleon. He crept back into France and raised another army.

JEAN-PIERRE: Oh, how I remember those hundred days when Napoleon came back. All the old army men, we were sure it was going to be like the old days.

HENRI: It didn't last long. The combined armies of Europe rushed to Belgium to meet Napoleon. The Battle of Waterloo in 1815 was Napoleon's last stand. The British Duke of Wellington proved to be the better general on that day. They didn't take any chances with Napoleon this time. They sent him all the way to the South Atlantic!

ALFONSE: You know, it's funny. Napoleon was so famous as a general. And he will probably be remembered for his

NAPOLEON'S EMPIRE

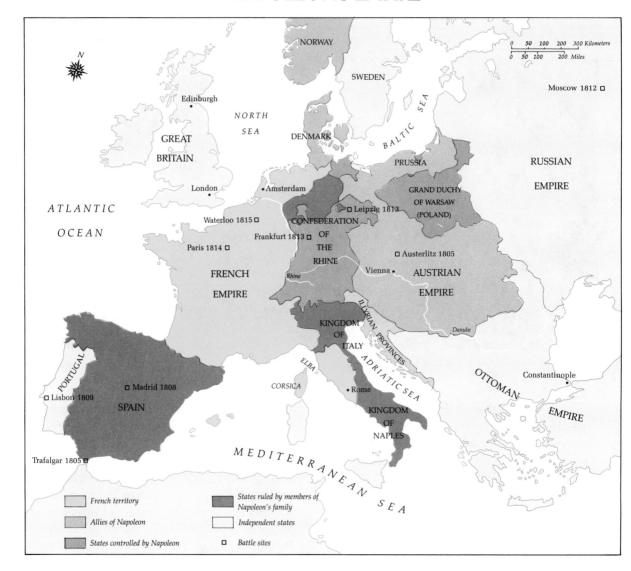

This map shows Europe at the time of Napoleon's empire and the sites and dates for some of his more important battles. Use the map to answer the following questions.

1. What was the easternmost land under Napoleon's control? The westernmost?

2. At what battle was Napoleon's fleet defeated off the coast of Spain?

3. What empire bordering Russia was allied with Napoleon?

4. At what battle in 1805 did Napoleon win his greatest land victory?

conquests. But I think his political accomplishments will prove to be the more lasting.

JEAN-PIERRE: What do you mean? Are you saying he wasn't a great military leader?

ALFONSE: Of course not. Even Henri here, who despises Napoleon, will admit to that. No, think for a minute about how Napoleon brought the achievements of the revolution into everyday life in France. First, look at the example of his own life. Napoleon believed that people's skills mattered, not their backgrounds or families. He changed things so that poor people had a chance to get ahead, in government, the army, business.

JEAN-PIERRE: Right. That's how I, the son of a peasant farmer, became an officer in the French army.

ALFONSE: For a military man who often made his own laws, he really did believe in law. The Napoleonic Code made laws the same all over France and for all the French people. He put an end to special treatment for the nobles.

JEAN-PIERRE: That's true. Someone once said that Napoleon combined the Enlightenment with the revolution. I think that's true He really did believe in new ideas, in finding the best way of doing things. He wasn't afraid of change. You're right, Alfonse. Napoleon really did change things. He brought many of the changes of the revolution to France and to the countries we conquered.

HENRI: I don't mean to interrupt your fond memories, but aren't you forgetting something? This was the man who trampled on law when it suited him. He was an emperor, maybe one with good ideas, but an emperor just the same.

ALFONSE: I agree with you, Henri, but I now realize he did many things that were good for France. What about you, Jean-Pierre?

JEAN-PIERRE: I don't know. Maybe I can only see the man as my commander. To serve with him was an honor I will remember all my life.

HENRI: Well, some of the French today will weep, and some will dance for joy. I wonder what the future holds for France?

✎ Quick Check

1. *Why was Napoleon chosen to lead France? How did the ideas of the revolution affect Napoleon?*

2. *What did Napoleon do in 1804? What happened to Napoleon at Waterloo? What was St. Helena?*

3. *How did his brothers benefit from Napoleon's rule of France? What plans did Napoleon have to drop because of the defeat at Trafalgar?*

4. *How did the people of Spain react to Napoleon's conquests of their country? What caused Napoleon's defeat in Russia?*

5. *Why might Napoleon be considered a hero by the poor people of France? How did France benefit from the Napoleonic Code?*

Review Skills and Exercises

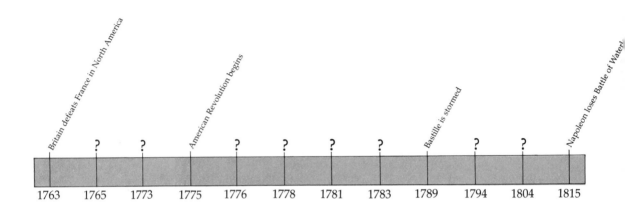

Timeline labels (top): Britain defeats France in North America, American Revolution begins, Bastille is stormed, Napoleon loses Battle of Waterloo

Timeline dates: 1763 1765 1773 1775 1776 1778 1781 1783 1789 1794 1804 1815

Putting Events in Order

You have just read about the American and French revolutions. Above is a time line giving dates and some events from Part 7. Each question mark stands for a missing event. Read the following list of events and study the time line to decide where each event belongs. Write the numbers 1–8 on a sheet of paper. Beside each number write the date where you placed the event. Refer to the text for help.

1. Battle of Yorktown is fought.
2. Reign of Terror ends.
3. Boston Tea Party is staged.
4. Colonists win Battle of Saratoga.
5. Stamp Act is passed.
6. Napoleon becomes emperor.
7. Treaty of Paris is signed.
8. American Declaration of Independence is written.

Reading Documents

A document is often used to make an official statement. The United States Constitution is such a document. During the French Revolution, the National Assembly adopted a document called the

Declaration of the Rights of Man. Below is an excerpt from a translation of that declaration. There is also an excerpt from another document, the American Declaration of Independence. Read the excerpts and answer the questions.

Declaration of the Rights of Man

The representatives of the French people, constituted as a National Assembly, considering that ignorance, forgetfulness, or contempt of the rights of man are the sole causes of public misfortunes and the corruption of governments, have resolved to set forth . . . the natural, inalienable, and sacred rights of man . . .

Men are born and remain free and equal in rights.

The purpose of all political association is the safeguarding of the natural . . . rights of man. These rights are liberty, property, security, and resistance to oppression.

The principal of all sovereignty resides essentially in the nation. Nobody, no individual, can exercise any authority which does not come from it.

Declaration of Independence

We hold these truths to be self-evident that all men are created equal, that they are endowed by their Creator with certain unalienable Rights, that among these are Life, Liberty, and the pursuit of Happiness.— That, to secure these rights, Governments are instituted among Men, deriving their just powers from the consent of the governed,—*That, whenever any Form of Government becomes destructive of these ends, it is the Right of the People to alter or to abolish it, and to institute a new Government.* . . .

1. Why are the Declaration of the Rights of Man and the American Declaration of Independence called documents?

2. What does the French document say are the rights of man? What does the American document say human rights include?

3. Each excerpt contains a sentence in italics. Explain what you think each sentence means.

4. What was going on in France and in the American colonies at the time each of these documents was written?

Building Vocabulary

The following words are taken from the excerpt above. Study the way each word is used in the documents. Then read the three possible definitions for each word. Write the numbers 1–6 on a sheet of paper. By each number write the word and the definition that best fits the word.

1. contempt
lack of respect for
appreciation
love

2. misfortunes
lotteries
unhappy events
taxes

3. security
wealth
freedom to worship
freedom from danger

4. endowed
provided with
helped
warned

5. deriving
giving
receiving
throwing away

6. institute
to keep forever
to establish
to provoke

GLOSSARY

absolute monarch. a ruler who has the right to make and break laws and rules with unquestioned authority.

alliance. a joining together of groups to promote their mutual interests.

anatomy. the study of the structure of the human body.

annul. to end a marriage by making it legally invalid.

apprentice. one who learns an art or trade by studying and working under a master.

archaeologist. one who studies cultures through the remains of tools, weapons, pottery, buildings, and writings.

artisan. a trained or skilled worker; a craftsworker.

bankruptcy. financial collapse or inability to pay one's debts.

baptism. a Christian ritual in which water is used to symbolize the admittance of an individual into the Christian community.

barbarian. a term used to describe an uncivilized person. It was used by the Romans to describe Germanic tribespeople.

battering ram. a large wooden pole with an iron tip. It was used to break down walls during a battle.

boyar. a Russian noble and landowner.

bubonic plague. a deadly disease that was common in Europe during the Middle Ages and Renaissance. It was spread by the bite of the Asian rat or its fleas.

caliph. title given to a type of Muslim ruler who usually controlled a large territory.

cathedral. a large church that was the seat, or headquarters, for a group of smaller parishes.

charter. a written agreement guaranteeing the rights and privileges of subjects in a state or country.

checks and balances. a system in which one branch of government limits the powers of another.

chivalry. the customs and behavior of the ideal medieval knight.

Christendom. the part of the world in which Christianity is the major religion.

citizen. a person who is loyal to a government and, in return, receives rights, privileges, and protection.

classics. Greek and Roman writings that were greatly admired during the Renaissance.

clergy. officials of a Christian church.

cockfight. a sporting event played with roosters.

colony. a territory over which a nation claims the right of possession and has political and economic control.

comedy. an amusing play that usually has a happy ending.

communion. a Christian ceremony in which bread and wine are taken in remembrance of the death of Jesus Christ.

compass. a device that indicates the direction of north.

conquistadore. the Spanish word for conqueror.

Counter-Reformation. a movement that fought against Protestant teachings and renewed interest in the Catholic Church.

courtly love. a medieval ideal of behavior and emotions for knights and their ladies.

crusade. a medieval military expedition intended to win the Holy Land from the Muslims.

czar. a Russian ruler with absolute power and authority.

Dark Ages. a term used to identify the period when Roman civilization broke down and feudalism developed; the early Middle Ages.

dauphin. the eldest son of the king of France.

divine right. the idea that a king receives the right to rule directly from God.

ellipse. an oval shape. Johanes Kepler discovered that the earth moved around the sun in an ellipse.

empire. a very large state or territory or a group of states ruled by a single government.

Enlightenment. a movement of European philosophers who promoted reason as a means of discovering truth.

estate. social group.

feudalism. a medieval political, social, and economic system. In a feudal society, there is no centralized government, but kings and nobles lend land and give favors in exchange for goods and services.

guild. a medieval association of merchants or artisans.

guillotine. a device used to kill people by cutting off their heads.

heir. one who inherits something.

heresy. the holding of beliefs which go against the teachings of the Catholic Church.

humanist. one who believes in the dignity and worth of the individual.

indentured servant. a person who agreed to work for an English colonist in exchange for passage to the English colonies.

Index. a list of books banned by the Catholic Church.

indulgence. a pardon for a sin, sold by Catholic clergy during the Middle Ages and Renaissance.

Inquisition. a campaign against beliefs which differed from Catholicism. In many cases it was a corrupt movement used to harass people, torture them, and steal their property.

interdict. a command from the pope that forbids a certain action.

Jacobin. a member of an eighteenth-century Parisian political club that defended the rights of the common people of France.

langue doc. a language native to southwestern France.

legend. a well-known story from the past that is often regarded as history.

manor. a medieval lord's land, usually worked by serfs.

masque. a short drama of the sixteenth and seventeenth centuries that was performed by masked actors.

medieval. a Latin word meaning "of the Middle Ages."

merchant. a buyer, seller, and trader of goods for profit.

microorganism. a living thing that is too small to be seen with the naked eye.

Middle Ages. the time period from about 500 to 1500, distinguished by a feudal society and a strong Christian Church.

model. example.

monarchy. a government headed by one ruler such as a king or queen.

monastery. a community of monks.

monastic rule. a common discipline for a group of monks.

monk. a male member of a religious order. In the Middle Ages they were devoted to serving God and preserving classical culture and Christian teachings.

mosque. a Muslim place of worship.

nation. a group of people united into a large political, economic, and social unit.

nationalism. a deep loyalty to one's country and culture.

nomadic. having no permanent town or village but instead wandering from place to place.

nun. a female member of a religious order, who devotes her life to serving God.

pagan. belief in more than one deity.

penance. an act of devotion, self-denial, or punishment designed to show repentance for sin.

philosopher. a person who studies ideas to gain a better understanding of life.

pilgrimage. in the Middle Ages, a journey to a holy place, such as Jerusalem.

plantation. a large farm, often worked by slave labor.

political science. the study of government.

pope. bishop of Rome and head of the Roman Catholic Church.

predestination. the belief that God determines what will happen to a person during his or her life and after death.

purify. cleanse.

Puritan. a member of a Calvinistic religious group in sixteenth- and seventeenth-century England. They lived according to a very strict moral code of behavior.

recant. to officially take back or renounce a statement or belief.

Reformation. a sixteenth-century religious movement resulting in the development of Protestantism.

Renaissance. a movement beginning in fourteenth-century Italy during which art and literature flourished.

repeal. cancel.

republican. a type of government in which the rulers are not monarchs but are chosen by the people or a select group.

revolution. the overthrowing of a government or ruler by the governed and then substituting another.

romance. a type of play that is neither comic nor tragic but attempts to show a wide range of human emotions and experiences.

Royalist. one who is loyal to the monarchy during a time when it is questioned.

sacrament. a formal religious ritual that is considered sacred or holy.

salon. a gathering of people in a private home to discuss ideas. In eighteenth-century France, they were usually organized by wealthy, well-educated women.

salvation. a liberation from sin and its effects.

scientific method. an organized procedure for gaining knowledge about something. It involves observing a subject, developing a theory, testing the theory, and forming a conclusion.

scurvy. a disease common to sailors on long sea voyages. It is caused by a lack of vitamin C, which is found in fresh fruits and vegetables.

sect. a religious group that follows a definite set of beliefs.

serf. a laborer who is legally bound to the land and subject to the will of an overlord.

siege. a military blockade of a city or town to force its people to surrender.

slave. a person who is owned by another person, either temporarily or permanently.

sonnet. a 14-line poem with a set rhyme scheme that was popular in the Renaissance.

superstition. a belief or practice resulting from fear, ignorance, or trust in magic and the supernatural.

surplus. more than is needed.

trade. buying, selling, or trading goods and services.

tragedy. a type of play in which a noble character clashes with a stronger force and loses.

transubstantiation. When a Catholic priest symbolically turns the communion bread and wine into the body and blood of Jesus Christ.

trial by ordeal. a test of guilt first used by Germanic tribespeople. A person accused of wrongdoing was forced into a dangerous situation or forced to endure bodily harm. If the person survived or if the injuries healed quickly, he or she was declared innocent.

troubadour. a type of poet-musician who entertained royalty and nobles in medieval France.

vassal. in a feudal society, a person who gives goods and services to a lord or king in exchange for protection.

wergild. a system of placing a cash value on a person. If someone was injured or murdered, the guilty person would pay this amount to the victim or victim's family. Based on Germanic tribal laws, it existed in the time of Charlemagne.

INDEX

253